A book for people who truly want to learn and grow...each step is so well planned out. So comprehensive. Wonderful moments of fun...easy fluid writing style.

-Barbara Wilder – Author of *Embracing Your Power Woman* and *Money is Love: Reconnecting to the Sacred Origins of Money*

Humor...wit and real stories, Lisa shares a simple and powerful approach to setting goals. Perseverance and resilience are part of the story, because sometimes life gets in the way and takes us down a different path, leading us back to where we started...so we can begin again.

-Andrea Hylen - *Author of Heal My Voice: An Evolutionary Woman's Journey. Creator of The Writing Incubator, on-line writing community. Founder of Heal My Voice*

Lisa's tools and processes will get and keep you on track. No matter what stage of life you're in, *A List is Not Enough* provides a clear and thoughtful roadmap to achieve your dreams.

-Ann Quasman - Founder, Creator and Former Host of *WomanTalk Live Radio* and *Conscious Conversations Café,* Founder, Creator and Former Facilitator of *Living in Your Heart* workshops.

...Loaded with eye openers. The Big Why, readiness, and the impact emotions can have on goal achievement were all extremely insightful. In short, if you're in goal planning mode this is a must read.

Mae Golden - Golden Business Processes

A List is not Enough:

A Modern Women's Guide to Better Goal Setting, Time Management and Productivity

Lisa Stearns

Stearns Coaching Publisher
Columbia, MD

Gratitudes

As the Mommas and the Papas song says, "This is dedicated to the one I love!"… to my partner, my soulmate, my best friend and my love. You are and always have been the wind beneath my wings. Thank you, thank you, thank you from the bottom of my very being, my dear sweet, husband Brad. I would never have made it to this glorious destination without you.

Other heartfelt Thank You's
If you ever want to feel gratitude, write a book. To those special friends who, through their continued support, check-ins, cheering, and loving encouragement, allowed me to arrive in this amazing place of accomplishment and fulfillment you are the light that kept me moving forward: Wendy Elover, Sherry Samuels, Pattie Robinson, Rob Robinson, Loraine Fray.

A special thanks to all those who volunteered to read this over their Thanksgiving holiday and give feedback and endorsements: Barbara Wilder, Andrea Hylan, Ann Quasman, Mae Golden,

Heartfelt thanks to my other Thanksgiving readers and sharers: BettyAnn Leesburg-Lange, Nirit Noddy, Roxanne Roloff,, Jamie Connelly, Sara Von Gunten (Amy's Mom), Lisa Gordon, and Vicky Harvey, Laura Betz, Angela Davids, Kat Stearns, Nancy Lewin, Bridgette Defrietas

Thanks to the many, many women of the Ms Biz Mornings Community, My Tribe, my heart, who have encouraged, supported and inspired.

My current Dream Team Mastermind™ Groups, and private clients who shared my dream with their network and made the success of this book possible.

To my editor, Donna Knutson, who patiently and lovingly agreed to let me be her first client.

To my beautiful friend and graphic designer, Josie Thompson, who is always so easy to work with, for her patience and creativity.

To Mary Gardella, the very talented photographer, who caught the me I feel like inside, but has never been captured on camera for my cover photo.

To my dad, who offered a lifetime of valuable lessons to learn, grow from and share.

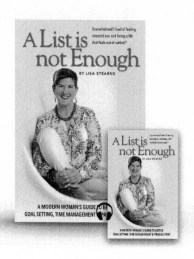

Download the AudioBook FREE!

READ THIS FIRST

Just to say thanks for buying my book, I would like to gift you the Audiobook absolutely FREE

Go Here to Sign up For the Download
https://www.lisastearns.com/audio.html

Game Changer Mornings

Blow Those Obstacles Away

Become that modern working woman with the highly rewarding life, right now.

Even if your current schedule is chaotic, your business lacks order, or you feel chronically overwhelmed, you CAN build strong new habits that result in living your best life.

With tools and experience across a variety of niches and professions, Lisa's programs are the most comprehensive resource you need to achieve your business and life goals.

GET STARTED TODAY!

Subscribe to Lisa's **Game Changer** Mornings
and get your first week FREE!

Based on the belief that the energy, focus and positivity you apply to the beginning of your day drives the quality of that day, the work you do and the life you lead, Game Changer Mornings gives you the optimal routine to begin each day. Each morning you'll receive a 5 minute recording which includes goal setting reminders and strategies, plus a guided, quiet moment to calm and clear your mind. You'll also receive a daily affirmation and beautiful journal page! Game Changer Mornings will transform your mornings from Chaos Central to Focus Fabulous!

Register here to say "YES" to creating your Game Changer Mornings www.LisaStearns.com/Home

About the Author

Business Coach for heart centered women, mindfulness teacher, and founder of Ms Biz Mornings networking organization, Lisa Stearns finds her days gloriously rewarding and filled with all the best life has to offer! Her previous work experiences include: owning a decorating franchise, being an American Council on Education (ACE) certified personal trainer, and selling men's suits (one of her favorite jobs), as well as creating Finding Your Voice Circles, a small public speaking groups for women.

She is most proud of having homeschooled her two sons, hiked 85 miles in the mountains of New Mexico with a full pack at age 54, been delightfully married to the same amazing man for 40 years and…having completed this book.

Lisa offers one to one business coaching, hosts Dream Team Mastermind™ groups, as well mindfulness and life mastery programs and retreats.

You can connect with Lisa immediately at www.LisaStearns.com or by tuning in to her weekly podcast, Just One Thing, where she and her husband of 40 years offer insight and encouragement to help you craft the life you desire by doing (you got it)… Just One Thing. You can find their podcast at http://JustOneThing.BuzzSprout.com

Section III Time Blocking

Section IV Work Life Integration:
The Mindfulness Connection

Section V Celebration

Section VI You Did It!

Section VII Resources & References

Preface

More than ever, today's modern woman is pulled in a thousand directions; career, family, community, relationships, teacher conferences, email, texting, meetings, pee wee softball. Yikes! Do you remember the last time you felt like you had 30 guilt free minutes where you focused on the things that were most important to you, and only you?

Great news! There is a book that answers all your burning "How do I do it all" problems in a creative, visual, easy to execute fashion. Filled with real life stories of people just like you, A List is Not Enough has been planned out and created to resolve your goal setting, time management, and productivity conundrums in a fun, playfully easy to read format. This book is for women who are tired of feeling overwhelmed, tired of living an over scheduled life and ready to craft a life that is calm, well ordered, productive and... rewarding.

As a life long lover of all things organized, a master of out-of-the-box thinking and a Queen of the art of breaking big ideas into manageable "bites," I have spent years voraciously consuming information by industry leaders in the area of Goal Success. My clients continued successes reflects that passion. Much like a kid in a candy shop, this stuff makes my heart soar! And, sharing it feels like sharing my favorite chocolate bar.

Career women, entrepreneurial mavens, and busy stay at home moms just like you, who struggle with the expectations of being a modern woman with an overflowing life have already successfully implemented these tool and been blown away by the changes in their lives.

Ann, an entrepreneurial photographer shared "Lisa's goal setting system has taught me so much about creating clear, achievable goals, having mile markers that remind me to celebrate the successes I have, and continually keeping my schedule manageable. Her system just makes sense!"

Based on the successes I have already seen with this program, I promise that if you follow along with this creative how-to workbook, you will be calmer, w-a-y more organized, have a significantly better handle on your schedule, and, (my bold promise), learn to love your self along the way.

There's no need to be the woman that's constantly frazzled, living on pop tarts, wearing mismatched socks and late to everything. You can be That Modern Take Charge Woman who knows where she wants to go and knows,.with clarity, how she is going to get there.

The tools your are about to read in A List is Not Enough have been repeatedly shown to slowly but surely rewire the way you think about your goals, your time and your life. These tools have permanently changed the lives of countless women just like you. All you have to do to begin your journey to a calmer, more manageable, fulfilling life is to keep reading. It's that simple.

Just.

Keep.

Reading.

Prologue

When I started this book I didn't realize how much life would get in the way. What began as a book about my goal setting system, quickly morphed into a personal journey, filled with obstacles, discoveries and lessons. The original draft of the book opened with how I've never considered myself a goal oriented person. But, as time passed and this writing project kept getting pushed to the back burner, I came to realize the importance of sharing my challenges in completing this book, which of course was my goal. Because, the reality is, that life keeps moving and obstacles get thrown in our way. The real gem of any goal setting system is that you have something clear and focused to keep coming back to... even when life is challenging.

The last five years of my life have been rife with health obstacles. Prior to this, I had been working hard to create the professional career of my dreams. I pursued the training I needed, had a healthy networking plan, did a lot of public speaking for locals organizations, and offered free classes, all in an effort to launch myself as a business coach.

Then, in 2014 my mother died, which triggered a series of disruptive events. As a result, anxiety and depression moved in like a Virginia creeper, slowly and steadily working its way into my body, mind and spirit. The ground was fertile; I had lived my whole life in overdrive. Exhausted and overwhelmed, a dark, sluggishness took root.

The anxiety and exhaustion made it almost impossible to leave the house. When I did manage to get out once a month to run my networking meeting, three to four days of recuperation were required, hours of which were spent on the couch in utter, bone weary, mind weary exhaustion.

Seeking some explanation for this exhaustion and anxiety, I consulted with myriad professionals. I was finally diagnosed with Post Traumatic Stress Disorder (PTSD), and Acute Adrenal Fatigue. The result was a better understanding of the source of my ever persistent weary, overwhelmed state, and how to move forward in a positive, powerful way.

With the help of Louise Hay's amazing book, *You Can Heal Your Life*, and a new found dedication to a hearty mindfulness practice, I was on my way. Combining her beautiful words, some yogic philosophy, and with the help of a truly gifted acupuncturist, my new focus and practice became navigating life with better respect for myself, my body, and my overall well-being. I created boundaries, which I'd never had before, and became a devotee of self-care. Life seemed to be on an upswing.

> **With a new found dedication to a hearty mindfulness practice, I was on my way.**

But, once again, life got in the way. I suffered a pretty serious concussion. It was devastating. It felt like all the work I'd done for the past two years had all been for naught! I suffered headaches, dizziness and chronic fatigue daily. Once again, my life became very small, the days filled with hours on the couch, and a rare 15 minute trip to a store. It was very disheartening and discouraging.

For almost a year I couldn't work on the computer or read at all. I couldn't create or draw. The days were a dreadful mix of frightening and boring in equal measure.

Sixteen months later, spring came with its new promise and I said, "Enough! I am going to walk myself well." And, I did.

I started out taking short walks on the paths in my neighborhood, gaining strength and resilience. I got to the point that I was walking 10+ miles per day. I started to feel like myself again.

With this renewed energy, I decided to dip my toe into mainstream life again. I tried adding coffee with friends to the calendar once a month. Sometimes it was fine. Sometimes it was still just too much. But, I persevered, determined to regain some form of my prior, highly engaged, physically active, socially fulfilling life. And, slowly but surely, I did.

The day finally arrived when I thought, "I'm ready...ready to attempt to relaunch my business." I joined a business networking and lead generation group. This was a huge commitment for me as it met every week and was a 20-40 minute drive away (20 minutes can be a harrowing drive during rush hour in the Baltimore/Washington corridor).

At the same time, and in support of the new launch, I decided to write this book. I felt I had finally come to better understand the true limits of my energy. I discovered how much I could and couldn't put in my schedule to continue my forward progress. I really thought I had found a new equilibrium.

> **For me, goal setting has
> always been logical.
> There are patterns and
> steps to follow that lead
> down a predictable path.
> As a coach, I have found
> that not everyone enjoys
> this clarity of thought.**

So, committed to this task, as I am with all undertakings, I set a schedule, found an accountability partner, and dedicated my free time to writing a book on goal setting, hoping to share my system with those who find goal setting a struggle.

For me, goal setting has always been logical. There are patterns and steps to follow that lead down a predictable path. As a coach, I have found that not everyone enjoys this clarity of thought.

That being said, like most people, I forgot to figure in the unexpected ups and downs of my life. What began as a methodical and logical approach ("I'll write a book outlining my goal setting system. No big deal.") ended up teaching me a great deal about life, stories, and why we don't always achieve that which we most desire.

In a nutshell, I still over did "it." I expected too much of myself. I put myself in situations that triggered a recurrence of PTSD episodes.

Life began to get sloggy (foggy + sluggish), again. The goal of writing a book dwindled and then faded.

From this brief telling, you may have noticed that I don't go down without a fight. I redoubled my efforts of mindfulness and self-care. I even took some training in Mindfulness Based Stress Reduction (MBSR).

I went on a seven day silent retreat, all the while wrestling with feelings of failure. That old label "You're Not Good Enough" and the crappy, tired story "You never finish anything" kept playing in the background.

Occasionally, and in times of high energy, positivity and clarity, I would laugh out loud seeing the humor in the situation. After all, how funny is it to set out to write a book about successful goal setting and not finish it? Hilarious, right?

It's now nine months since I last worked on this book. My health is on the upswing again. I'm stronger, smarter, and more cautious with my time, boundaries, energy and expectations. I'm also much smarter about goal setting, what it looks like for me, feels like for me, and how to proceed when life gets in the way.

It's important to note to you readers that the balance I found is one that worked for me. I needed to learn my obstacles, strengths, and struggles to be able to move forward with this big goal. The balance you find is going to be unique to you. It is going to require trial and error and the perseverance to keep showing up. This book provides the tools; the journey is completely yours.

My hope is that you will find direction, focus, tools and a good healthy dose of reality from this book. You will become more mindful and remember to celebrate. Goal setting can be very black and white, very linear. The process of Goal Getting can be messy and confused, fraught with ups and downs, unforeseen obstacles and life changing lessons. At the same time, with planning, determination and resilience, you will reach the ultimate goal…

SUCCESS!

May you enjoy the process as much as I did and find the answers you are seeking.

Lisa

My Other Prologue

If you'd asked me 10 years ago, if I was goal oriented, as my husband frequently did, you would have consistently heard a resounding, "No."

I don't recall ever having detailed, long term projections of things to come. I don't remember thinking, "A year from now this is what my life will look like. " Or, "Six months from now I want to have done…". I didn't make lists or keep a journal. I just showed up and things happened.

My life was, and always had been, a series of seemingly spontaneous decisions, generally requiring some form of immediate action to solve an urgent or pressing problem or to achieve a desired result. I operated in the "now." If there were bumps in the road, I took them in stride expecting that I could handle whatever popped up, trusting that the objective, in some form, would be realized. Or not. Some goals were not achieved; but without much thought or reflection, I just moved on.

As I write this, I am aware of how simplistic and maybe, naive this sounds. But, it is how my mind worked, my system…how I navigated life.

Overall, it worked. I knew that I wanted certain things: to be married, to have kids and to have a job. But, when I thought about goal setting, the process that came to mind had "To Do" lists, calendars and planning stuff. (I'm not even sure what that means, but trust me, there were piles and folders requiring a good deal of sorting.) My approach appeared to me to have no planning, no forecasting, no lists or milestones? More importantly, what I soon came to realize was most lacking in my approach was a time to enjoy the feeling of success or accomplishment that is supposed to accompany a completed goal. Hmmm,... no celebrations? That can't be right. Can it?

If I didn't set goals how did I get anything done?

Like a thorn in my sock, this question scratched and scraped at me. I had to know the answer. Was I a person that didn't set goals? If so, how did I get anything done?

Hounded by questions and with a driving curiosity, I began to read about the history, anatomy and science of goals. I learned what differentiates a goal from a wish or a dream. I began to form a picture of all the bits and pieces of goal setting, follow through, and success, that separate the random achievers from the truly, consistently successful. It was empowering and exciting. You see, I love making order out of chaos, whether it's mine or that of others, and this goal setting and goal getting process that I was researching did exactly that.

In my search, I came to understand my own goal setting style, and why I never felt successful after achieving a goal. My inability to feel successful and the subsequent path of self-discovery ended up unraveling and repairing a life long pattern of Not Good Enough Syndrome and a lack of self-love.

Through this journey of research and self-discovery, I began to listen more closely as people talked about their goals; and I was quickly able to pinpoint what was standing in their way; and, because of my journey, I was able to help them experience a feeling of accomplishment and success. There's tons of science I could share here. But, for simplicity's sake, let's just say success breeds more success, that's how the brain works.

I felt like I had found the key to Goal Setting and Goal Getting Nirvana and now desperately wanted to share. I wanted to show people how easy it could be to go from being a Goal Dreamer, with occasional and random success, to a serial Goal Getter, one who could not only set clear, attainable goals, but who could understand the process so well that it was easily repeatable.

More than anything, I wanted people to experience the joy of success, that heart flipping feeling that begins as a flutter in your stomach and bubbles up into your throat making you want to laugh out loud with wonder and delight.

This passion and clarity fueled the motivation to write this book. I want to share a process that helps you create Good Goals, ones that are clear, concise and attainable. Equally important, I want you to be able to put an end to chronic overwhelm, disappointment and ineffective list-making.

Equally important, I want to provide the tools that help unlock the mysterious roadblocks that may be preventing your progress and finally bring a sense of calm orderliness to your life…to slow life down.

Moreover, I want to help you create a habit of celebration to help you pause and relish the success of a task accomplished, of a milestone met, of a goal completed. I want to help you learn to continually pause long enough to say, "I'm wonderful! I did it!", before careening off toward the next goal!

Imagine how amazing it will be to have a roadmap to victory, a path so easy to follow that success is a given. Wouldn't that be worth a few hours of your time? You bet!

I want to help you create a habit of celebration. To help you pause and relish the success of a task accomplished, of a milestone met, a goal completed.

Section 1

Goal Setting

How To Use This Book

True change happens in small steps, big goals or tasks broken down into smaller, more manageable bits. Research shows it takes a minimum of 21 days to create a new habit. The concept of this book is to create new habits. These tools will take time and practice to make your own.

A good friend of mine, a professional organizer, told me that the majority of her large library of organizing books came from her clients who had bought them but never gotten around to using them. In that light, I'm going to ask you to take this book in nibbles. Feel free to read it from cover to cover and then cherry pick one section to work on. Or, you can read just one section and master those tools before moving on.

If, at any time, you find yourself thinking this is just too much, don't despair. To help you keep it manageable, you will find a "Great Ways to Break It Down " checklist at the end of each section that gives you daily, useful practices you can employ to master the bigger skill. Believe it or not, these checklists are where you will identify and begin to change the habits that are having the biggest negative impact on your life.

> **Through tiny changes come BIG results**

Included in each section, you will also find Coaches Comments, as well as a Troubleshooting Guide containing questions that I most frequently encounter from my clients and possible answers for you to consider.

Finally, growth can't happen without reflection. Each section has insightful questions to better help you understand your current thoughts about each subject area. When you understand the stories your mind is telling you are empowered to make smart, rational, informed choices and change.

Welcome aboard! As one of my new clients, together we will take all of these tools in small nibbles. You will get lots of feedback, encouragement, refining, reminding, clarifying, and even be held accountable, as you progress. Allow yourself time to make these tools yours. Be kind and patient. If you do, I promise the result will be a more manageable life and a very deep feeling success.

Watch for Coaches Comments...

Each section in this book contains very detailed instructions, exercises and trouble shooting guidance. These are the same exercises and trouble shooting I use with my coaching clients. Through trial and error, and continued tweaking, we make sure the steps involved are always manageable.

Because you are not here in person, I can't foresee or anticipate your personality, your influencers, your motivators and learning style. I don't know you, but, you know you. So, I am coaching you now, reminding you to customize the tools to best fit your needs.

Feel free to adjust each practice to make it your own. Play with the concepts and tweak them to meet your needs, strengths and struggles. Although the topic is Goal Setting and Goal Getting, this is really a sojourn into self-discovery.

Here's to the journey!

Reflections About Reading This Book

What fears do you have about Goal Setting, Prioritizing and Time Blocking? What can you do to ease these fears?

_____

_____

What words or phrases did you hear in your mind while reading this section, or when thinking about reading a book about Goal Setting and Time Management.

_____

_____

Do you believe that you are unable to improve your abilities in any of these areas? Does one area, Goal Setting, Time Blocking or Prioritizing, stand out more than the others? If so, why?

_____

_____

If so, I invite you to open your mind to the possibility that you already have abilities you don't know about in each of these areas. And, it is these hidden talents that you and I are going to turn into Super Powers!

A List is Not Enough
or It's Right Here in My Hat

 As I continued to study the topic of goal setting and success, and as I compared it to how I had achieved things in my life, I rapidly realized two things. First, because up to this point goals appeared with complete clarity in my head, meaning the entire process from conception to completion, I had no idea there were so many steps involved to be successful, and so many tiny places for one to get lost and fail.

Second, I began to ponder, were there specific tools required for success? Was list-making one of them? List- making always seemed to be a big part of goal setting for those I observed. But, I have known several chronic list-makers who seem to achieve very few of their goals? This lead me to wonder was it the list, or the list-maker that was the source of the struggle? If list-making didn't guarantee some kind of success, what was the purpose of making one? I admit, I was a bit confused.

I can't imagine a more perfect example of the disconnect between list-making and actually getting things done than this simple story involving my son. Today, he is a highly successful project manager for a major consulting firm, and even he gets a kick out of this story.
One summer, when he was seven, I was making all the usual preparations for a family vacation. With a million things still to be done before we could leave, I told him there were three tasks he needed to do to get ready. 1. Unstack the dishwasher, 2. Take out the kitchen trash and 3. Collect some toys for the trip.

31

Now, knowing my son had both a vivid imagination and a colossal lack of focus, I gave him a list, explaining the importance of getting these tasks done without my having to nag him. Always eager to please, he confidently replied, "No problem, Mom."

An hour and a half later I became aware of a distinct lack of noise, the kind of noise made by a young boy doing chores.

I started calling his name trying to figure out where he could be. Receiving no response to my entreaties inside the house, I put my head out the door wondering if he had ended up outside seeking some special toy.

"Easton?" I called. "Where are you?"

In a sing-songy voice he replied, "Out here, Mom. On the swing. It's so peaceful out here."

"That's lovely sweetheart," I replied. Confused by the fact that he was playing and not doing his tasks I continued, "But, where is your list, honey?" (Wait for it...)

He patted his head and exclaimed, "Right here in my hat, mom!" Then, he continued to swing.

Right here in my hat. Perfect! How many times do we make a goal, even make a list, only to put it aside as though the list-making itself somehow accomplishes the goal? Then, we find ourselves wondering why our lives, or circumstances haven't changed. We feel like a failure because we aren't where we thought we would be. This list-making disconnect is one of the key reasons our goals remain nothing more than dreams and wishes. We list and we imagine, but we forget to Do.

Learning how to move from list to action is a skill that requires practice. Setting the goal is just the first step.

Understanding both the tools and steps required to convert goal setting to Goal Getting is something very few people talk about, or teach. Yet, this process is an essential element for creating success. For some reason, we all just assume, like me, that goals simply happen. And, when they don't we are confused and disappointed.

Before You Set a Goal:
Your Pre-Goal Assessment

There are several steps that every successful person takes, whether they know it or not, that allows them to; create clear, attainable goals, achieve them, and have a feeling of success upon their completion.

Let's begin by looking at what I call your pre-goal assessment. It includes:

1. Stating/writing your goal
2. Asking "Why this goal?"
3. Exploring your readiness
4. Refining your goal with clarity and purpose

As you are reading this I can hear you thinking "Is all this really necessary? This seems like a ton of stuff!" The answer is yes, if you want to be repeatedly successful.

A goal without a plan is a wish

Here's what I discovered about myself and others that I have coached. If you don't understand the totality of the Goal Setting / Goal Getting process, I guarantee you are going to miss out on something really, really important.

For me, in the past, since I didn't understand my process, I missed out on finding any joy, or a sense of accomplishment in my achievements. This was the missing piece in the Goal Getting process, for me. Rewarding myself. For you, it might be something else. Which is why I feel so strongly about understanding and embracing what I refer to as goal anatomy...all the inner workings of Goal Getting. The pre-goal assessment is just one of the critical pieces of this goal anatomy.

With this book, you will build habits and practices that will slow life down and make you a "naturally" successful Goal Getter. You will come to recognize the areas of your process that need special attention: an accountability partner, outside help, a better list, a pause for celebration...whatever it is <u>you</u> need.

Again... the answer to the question, is this assessment really necessary, is a resounding "yes!" If you want to be certain that when you set a goal you succeed, then you need to understand where your strengths and struggles lie and proactively create an action plan for success.

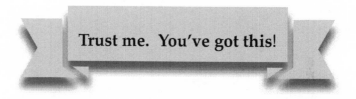

Trust me. You've got this!

Let's Get Started :
The BIG Why

As I continued to read and explore the topic of goals and success, one theme seemed to keep surfacing as an essential starting place, what's frequently referred to as The Big Why. Meaning, why is this goal important to you.

I read one of the best illustrations of "The Big Why" concept in Napoleon Hill's book *Think and Grow Rich*. To demonstrate the importance of this idea, he shares a story of one of his first coaching clients whose goal was to be rich.

Together they created a plan that would expand his business in two years, exponentially increasing his income in a short period of time.

The man's business grew as projected. The money came rolling in. About 9 months later, Napoleon Hill asked, "How's it going?"

With a shake of his head, his client responded, "Terrible!" He went on to say, "The money is rolling in but, all I do is work. I don't have any free time."

Confused, Mr. Hill asked, "Wasn't your goal to be rich?"

The man replied, "Well, no... what I really wanted was to travel."

When creating his goal, this client forgot to answer the most important and defining question. Why do you want this goal?

In his case, the Big Why should have been, why do you want to be rich? In the client's mind, a person needs money to travel. He didn't have enough money. Therefore… well, you see the problem. Wanting to be rich, and wanting to travel are completely different goals requiring completely different plans.

Let's make sure you start out on the right path by exploring your Big Why and assure the goal that you set is the goal you really want to achieve. It's no good to work a million hours to make a million dollars if what you really want is to visit Venice!

Woo-Hoo! Look at you, getting ready to ask the hard questions, trying new things, *and* then doing the work! Time to celebrate your amazing-ness. You are one dynamic woman!

State Your Goal:
Step 1 Getting Your Goal on Paper

It's time to take action and write down a goal. Don't worry how big it is, how small it is, whether it's business or personal, or how it's worded. We will work on that as we go, and your goal stating abilities will naturally improve with time and practice.

The following pages are designed to help you understand your goals mindset, your process, where your invisible obstacles lie, and more.

Begin by Stating Your Goal

Identify three goals in any area of your life. A goal is simply something you want to accomplish.

Example:
"I want to spend more time with my husband." Or, "I want to increase my sales by 30% by next year."

We will continue to refine your goal stating throughout this book. Right now, you are learning how Visual Goal Mapping™ works. Don't get bogged down in choosing the perfect goal to work on. Pick the top three that come immediately to mind.

Goal 1

_____

_____

Goal 2

_____

_____

Goal 3

_____

_____

Now, arbitrarily choose one goal. Note: you will get the most benefit from this exercise if you choose a goal that has some complexity, uncertainty and a wee bit of emotion; fear, anxiety, concern, etc.

Troubleshooting Goal Stating

This whole book is dedicated to Troubleshooting the process of writing clear, achievable goals. Therefore, I'm not going to add any Troubleshooting comments here. I just encourage you to keep on reading.

You're doing great. Take a moment to do a little "I'm rockin' it" dance.

Now, you are ready to move on to step 2...

THE **BIG** WHY
Step 2

In order to achieve your goal you must understand as much as possible about it. This includes your motivation, the impact it may have on your life, your relationships, your current schedule, and more. Some of these influencers, like lack of clarity, finances, current obligations, or certain relationships can be a primary source of hidden obstacles. Answering the following questions will provide laser focus, assuring that you are going after the right goal, for the right reasons, at the best possible time.

1. Where did this idea/goal come from? What inspired this idea?

_____

_____

2. What need is going to be met by accomplishing this goal?

_____

_____

3. Once accomplished, how will your life be be changed?

_____

_____

4. What emotion or state of mind will be produced by achieving this goal?

_____

_____

5. Who else in your personal or work life will be impacted by this goal?

_____

_____

5a. Will this person(s) support this goal? Y / N / I haven't talked with them about it.

6. Is there another/different goal that can more easily or quickly get you to the same end result? If yes, go back to #1.

_____

_____

7. Re-examine your answers and ask, "Is this the correct goal?" Is there something that doesn't feel right?

_____

_____

Continue to tweak your goal until all of your answers:

1. Come from an authentic place (meaning this feels really comfortable in your gut with no outside influencers.) *Please note, this may absolutely be the right thing to do *and*, at the same time, it may make you really nervous, or afraid. It's still the right thing to do.

2. Are your goals clear and specific enough to be energizing with a sense of direction and purpose. We will cover how to be more specific as we continue. For now, keep in mind the story of the

client who thought he wanted to be rich when, in fact, he really wanted to travel.

One of my favorite client "ah-ha" moments came during a workshop I hosted for a university leadership program. Participants had listed their three goals and were moving on to their Big Why. As I surveyed the room scanning for any indications of confusion, or "stuck-ness" my eyes landed on Sarah, a mid-thirties, eager, energetic, highly professional looking woman.

We had made it as far as question 5, "Who will be affected by this goal?", when a look of real confusion came over her face. When I asked if she needed help, she proceeded to detail her three main goals for the immediate future.

She said, "Goal 1 is to go back to college for my masters. Goal 2 is to run for public office. And, Goal 3 is to spend more quality time with my husband."

She paused with obvious reflection. She replied, "I really want to go back to school. It's important for my career and my desire to run for local office. But, both of those goals are going to have a huge impact on my husband, as he will have to watch the kids more, not to mention cut into any chance of us spending more quality time together."

She continued, "I guess I never really considered that these three goals are mutually exclusive. I can't have more quality time with Gary if I go back to school, unless I change my work schedule."

> **Many of us have hundreds of goals floating around in our head that simply aren't compatible, and we just can't see it.**

Although Sarah's realization is obvious from the outside looking in, many of us have hundreds of goals floating around in our head that simply aren't compatible, and we just can't see it. One goal cancels out the other due to time, money or other constraints in our rather full lives.

It isn't until we pause, create a list all of our goals (life, career, personal, health, financial) in one place, and ask the Big Why questions that we get a complete picture of what's possible and what's not. Once written, we can consider our schedules, our partners, our overall well-being, our finances, etc., and take a well-informed look at what is realistic and what's not, what needs to be put on the back burner or pitched once and for all. It is the best way to create clear goals and have clear expectations with any confidence that you will succeed.

Noted author C. A. Woolf says, "What has been seen cannot be unseen, what has been learned cannot be unknown." Once known, we have the power of choice and positive action. When we clear our minds of conflicting goals, then we can truly focus on those that will move us toward the life we really want to live.

Make the time to ask the Big Why questions about your goals, especially the bigger goals, like having a child, changing careers, moving, taking on an extra job, or working a project that requires a lot of travel.

The knowledge you glean will be well worth the effort, and it will assure that you are moving forward with clarity in the best possible direction.

Yow-zah! You are knocking this Your Big Why thing out of the park! You're taking small steps and being kind to yourself. Way to go!

Troubleshooting Your Big Why

My goal involves others. What do I do?

When we are working with someone on a project or goal the outcome is not solely our responsibility. In this case, the best choice is to fill out the Big Why together, assuring you are both on the same page across the board.

Next, create very clear and specific expectations (using the SMART goal guidelines outlined further in this book) for each task.

Then, discuss what to do when deadlines aren't met.

Finally, and most importantly, realize right from the start that you are not in this alone and that you can only do your part.

I change my mind or lose interest a lot. Any suggestions?

I refer to this as Shiny Object Syndrome. Like a crow, some of us are very easily distracted by the next new pretty thing, instead of being content with what's already in our nest, meaning our existing goal.

If you are highly creative, or have difficulty focusing, this may be the time to consider some brain training, otherwise known as mindfulness.

You can begin your brain training with as few 30 seconds a day, adding more time as you feel more confident and time allows. A wonderful mindfulness practice for the beginner could be simply focusing on where you notice your breath in your body.

When your mind wanders to new thoughts, gently bring yourself back to your breathing experience. For more ideas see the Mindfulness Section in this book or check out the free app version of Insight Timer, available on the App Store or Google Play.

The take away is, when your brain starts to dance with the lure and excitement of a new idea, continue to direct your attention back to the goal you have already set for yourself. Using a checklist like this may help:

☐ Does this new goal help achieve my original goal?
☐ If I pursue this new "shiny object" what will happen to my old goal?
☐ Do I have time to do both?
☐ Do I need to be attempting two big goals at the same time?

There is nothing wrong with new sparkly ideas. They are only a problem if they are constantly derailing you from the greatness you could be achieving right now by remaining fully committed to the goal you've already started. (More about what to do with Great Ideas that just pop into your head later.)

 I thought I knew what I wanted, now I'm not so sure.

Getting to your real Why takes practice. It asks us to think deeply, beyond the obvious, beyond the initial response.

The most successful people make allowances for the unexpected and their own evolving aspirations. The best recommendation I can make is to go ahead and stick with your initial goal in its original form. Then, come back to it a few times continuing to ask the Big Why questions; be open to something new or more specific as it presents itself. Continue asking the questions until all the answers feel solid, comfortable and clear. Trust your gut.

 I'm pretty sure an important person in my life does not support this choice. What do I do?

This is a tough one. I'm not going to sugar coat it. I do know that any resolution begins with a conversation where you are genuinely willing to listen to their objections and concerns.

Be prepared to state the benefits and possible challenges without:

- anger
- frustration
- judgement

Next, look for places where both of your views overlap or where you have common ground. Can you compromise or choose a slightly different path that would be acceptable? If you were offering another person possible solutions, other than yours, what might they be?

Finally, be prepared to examine this goal without their support. What does that look like? What other support do you need or could you find? If this goal is a Game Changer (more on Game Changers later) for you, what small step can you take to begin to make it happen on your own?

The Big Why:
Great Ways to Break It Down

Overwhelmed by the idea of working through all 8 steps of the Big Why worksheet every time a new goal comes up? *Chill-lax!*

Below is a list of different options you can use to break down your Big Why. Read through the whole list. Choose one that most appeals to you. Get comfortable with it by practicing several times a day for a week. Then, if you want, move on to another. If you don't like a practice, feel free to drop it and choose a new one. Any one of these small practices will still reap big rewards. And, remember, this is all about you.

1. When a new goal comes to mind, choose just one question from the Big Why worksheet and allow time for deep consideration. Focus on feelings. How does thinking about this make you feel? Do you notice any sensations in your body?

2. When thinking about a new goal, practice considering other goals you are already working on. Is there time for a new goal in your schedule?

3. Practice pausing before saying "yes" to another obligation, project or committee. Just pause and ask, "Do I really want to do this? Does this serve my greater good" (my future me and those I love). The best way to create that pause is to make a habit of responding to requests for your time with a simple statement like, I have to check my calendar. I'll let you know tomorrow.

4. Practice saying "no" (these may seem the same but are actually very different). Saying no can take great courage. Be prepared with an affirmation like, "I am a good person. Saying "no" is an act of self-care and will make me a more patient, more present, better rested person for those in my life." Remember, if you are confident with Your Big Why answers, you have designated a particular goal as a Game Changer. Each activity you say yes to takes time away from a goal that you have labeled as a top priority.

5. Choose a Big Why question and focus on clarity. Do you need to refine your goal or change it completely? Refer back to the story of the gentleman who really wanted to travel, but mistakenly created a goal of making more money. If you want to travel, then travel is the goal.

6. Observe when the words "should do" run through your mind or come out of your mouth. Frequently "should do's" have old stories attached to them, things your parents, teachers or other Influencers from your childhood imposed upon you. Just notice them.

7. Practice replacing "should do's" with "if I wanted to I could…". By doing so you will create space to have a choice verses responding out of the "should do" habit.

   For example, you've had a chaotic week at work and are feeling overextended and frazzled. The thought pops into your head "Shoot. It's my turn to bring snack tomorrow. I *should* bake homemade cookies. That's what a good mom would do."

Whoa there, Buckaroo! "Should do" Alert! Time to push pause and replace "I Should bake cookies…" with, "If I wanted to bake homemade cookies, I could. *But, does that really work for me right now?*" In this case, the answer is a hearty, "No!" You are tired and frazzled. The kids will be fine with store bought snacks. And, you need the rest.

When I decided to eliminate "should do's" from my life, I replaced "should do" with "Does this activity serve my greater good?" Sometimes the answer was yes, other times, no. The answer didn't matter. It was the freedom created by asking that question.

The simple practice of asking, "Does this serve my greater good?" gave me the ability to make a new decision with a fresh perspective. It freed me from guilt, obligation and negatively patterned behavior. For the first time in my life I had a choice.

It doesn't matter what cue you choose to use. The important thing is to be aware of when you are automatically reacting to "I should…" By raising your awareness, you can create a practice that allows for choice.

Reflections on The Big Why

Take a moment to reflect on your Big Why and jot down any additional thoughts, concerns, or "ah-ha's" you want to remember. Don't overthink it. Just let it flow.

What concerns came up? What one thing can you do to address *one* of these concerns?

_____

_____

What words, phrases or whole sentences did you hear in your mind while working on your Big Why?

_____

_____

Did you have an Ah-ha moment? If so, describe it in detail.

_____

_____

_____

Are you experiencing anxiety or frustration in reference to Your Big Why? Would it be possible to let go of what is causing you worry and focus on just one of the Great Ways to Break It Down activities? Which activity seems like it would be easiest or most interesting to try?

_____

_____

Write one positive comment about yourself and your ability to make good decisions. If you get stuck try: I have made many good decisions in the past like the time I...

_____

_____

Changing your mindset with an affirmation:

> *I am ready and open to ...*

Coaches Comment:
New to affirmations? They are simple to create and magically transform your life if you follow a few rules. Rule #1, affirmations are always stated in the present; I am, I have, I discover, I create, I let go of... Rule #2, it's best to avoid words with a negative connotation, words like can't, not, won't and don't. Here's some suggestions to get your started this time around: I am ready and open to...
>> *...change how I see myself.*
>> *...new opportunities.*
>> *...create the life I desire.*

You've stated your goal, and, asked Your Big Why. Now it's time to move on to step 3.

Wait a minute… did you remember to celebrate a job well done? It's never too late to pause and pat yourself on the back. Do a dance. Give yourself a high five! That was some inspiring work you just did!

Are You Ready?
Step 3

I recently saw a Facebook poster that said, "We all waste a lot of time waiting until we're ready. No one's ever ready. There's no such thing as ready. There's just now." I have a love - hate relationship with this quote. Here's why.

For those who are genuinely ready, meaning those who have done the research, taken the training, and prepared with some diligence, the message is perfect. It is simply, quit sitting around waiting for everything to be perfect and as Nike says, "Just do it." Within this context, there is a certain simplicity, beauty and power in the sentiment, there is just now.

> **No one's ever ready. There's no such thing as ready. There's just now.**

All too frequently, we have adequately prepared. Then, instead of beginning the project, we go into a semipermanent stall phase, creating a shopping list of things that have to happen before we can take The Leap. If you have done the work, you're ready. Trust yourself to boldly move forward with your goal. If a challenge arises, you can always ask for help, research that specific circumstance, or, hire a coach or other professional. With any new endeavor, unforeseen circumstances will arise. Count on it *and* know, deep in your inner being, that whatever arises you will come through a smarter, wiser person.

But, what about when you genuinely are not ready? What if you haven't taken the training you needed, haven't asked the professionals, don't have the support system in place, and haven't done the research? Sadly, this can happen. You think you're ready, but you're not. You have an abundance of courage or confidence. You take The Leap and crash, which frequently results in a feeling of failure.

Let's stop right there. Time for a pause. The only reason I included a discussion on Readiness is to address this idea of failure. Being courageous enough to jump into the unknown is a Super Power. There is no failure here. There are only lessons to be learned. When you look past the fact that you didn't achieve the desired outcome, frequently all that remains is the reality that you weren't adequately prepared. You weren't ready.

A lack of Readiness is easily remedied by focusing your Super Power on preparations. Courageously ask successful business owners how they got started, ask other new moms who have re-entered the work force what their secret is to a healthy schedule. Be bold in your pursuit of the answers you need. Once you've done your

Be bold in your pursuit of the answers you need.

due diligence, go back to those same one or two successful people and ask them to review your new plan for any holes, places you may still need to do some work to create the outcome you are seeking.

A final note on your Super Powers. They should never be viewed as a negative. You may need to learn to monitor yourself, being aware of the energy this Super Power can have over your better judgement. When you feel that energy is engaged, find a trusted mentor and ask for feedback on your Readiness. Much like Spider Man's web shooting hands, when you decide to let your power loose, you want to be sure you are releasing it in the appropriate time and at the correct target.

The first time I learned of the Readiness scale, it was many years back in my training as an American Council on Exercise (ACE) personal trainer. The text book referenced it as an important tool for the trainer in creating a clients wellness journey. The examples they shared were in reference to those looking to quit smoking or lose weight. But, I immediately saw its value in trying to achieve any goal.

As a personal trainer, it is important to be aware of your client's preparedness, commitment and more, so that you can set realistic expectations. Armed with this insight, you can inform your client about areas that need more work, education or support. You can also create a program built around small, manageable steps, filled with opportunities for growth and ultimate success.

So, as it relates to your business, your life, your overall well being, after Your Big Why, the next critical question is... "Are you really ready for your goal?"

Here is what the actual Readiness Chart looks like. (The fancy name is below the chart.) It's a good idea to read through it and familiarize yourself with the stages. This understanding will support you as you move forward with any goal; because, you can gauge where you are; what you still need to do; and you can proceed accordingly with more confidence in your ability to achieve your desired outcome.

Whenever I think about Readiness, I think about my client Nancy, a new health coach, who definitely wasn't...ready. She came to me feeling overwhelmed, stressed and unable to get her schedule under control. Nancy described herself as 'flighty' and 'all over the place.' We discussed options, small steps she could take to reduce her stress and bring some calm and order into her life. After three sessions Nancy hadn't been able to implement any of the micro-steps we had come up with. She knew she needed to change. She even really wanted to change. She just couldn't seem to make it happen.

Five Stages of Readiness
1. **Pre-contemplation** ~ You don't have any intention of changing your behavior to include this new goal in the next six months.
2. **Contemplation** ~ You are aware of the need to change in the next six months but lack commitment.
3. **Preparation** ~ you've decided to change and have a contemplated a plan.
4. **Action** * WINNER!! You have made specific changes in the past six months to reach this goal. *Note: Those that reach stage four are highly likely to accomplish their goal.
5. **Maintenance** ~ You have executed the desired change for six months *and* you have a plan to prevent relapse.

(*Trans-theoretical Model of Behavioral Change Prochaska & DiClemente, 1983*)

Nancy was at Stage 2 on the Readiness Chart. She was very aware of the chaos her current choices were creating, and the negative impact her schedule was having on her life. She even wanted the change. She just wasn't ready. Nancy wasn't a bad person, lazy or lacking the desire to change. She just wasn't ready to make the commitment.

We worked on building her confidence, breaking tasks down to smaller, more manageable action steps, and incorporating mindfulness activities. In a few weeks, Nancy was able to take the first important step toward a more calm, orderly schedule. She made it to Step 4. Way to go Nancy!

Now, it's your turn. Look at the Readiness Chart and honestly (honestly) assess where you are right now with respect to your goal. This simple assessment will save you lots of time, energy and heartache.

Once you assess your readiness you can see what the next step is and prepare. Or, ditch this goal altogether. The beauty is… it's totally up to you and within your power. The choice is yours, free from shame, embarrassment, failure, feelings of overwhelm and confusion. The Readiness Chart is just a tool. Use it to inform and educate. Then, plan accordingly.

Troubleshooting Your Readiness

 I think I'm ready and committed, but I seem to stop and start a lot, then lose momentum. What am I doing wrong?

This is a common complaint. So, don't think it's only you. Most times when "stutter-starting" is a problem it means one of two things.

First, your goal may be too big. Break it down into smaller, easier tasks, *especially* if fear is getting in the way. Breaking it down in the Readiness phase usually means you need:

- More education or training
- More support, sometimes professional
- Smaller, simpler steps

Example:
If you want to start doing presentations but you are terrified of public speaking, your *initial* goal can't be "Give a 30 minute presentation to my club." That needs to be broken w-a-y down... because you're not ready. You're terrified!

Break this goal into smaller, more manageable tasks. Your list should look more like this:

1. Write a one minute talk.
2. Practice it for two weeks until it flows from my mind without thought, like when someone asks my favorite flavor of ice cream.

3. Invite three friends over for tea and ask them to listen and give only positive feedback.
4. CELEBRATE my huge success!
5. Write a three minute talk. (Repeat steps 2-5.)

I believe asking the following question really helps here: "If I'm not ready for..., what am I ready for?" Give yourself permission to start with tiny tasks and build up. "Trial by fire" is rarely the best scenario for success.

Huge goals and Readiness are definitely interrelated. Big goals generally require big change, more preparation, more skills, and more experience. You've heard the old question, "How does one eat an elephant?" The answer, "One bite at a time." Give yourself permission to make ridiculously small changes that you *are* ready for and you'll find commitment and follow through much easier.

We will be doing a lot more work on breaking down your goals in the coming pages. Hang in there and just keep going..

So, back to the question:

 I think I'm ready and committed, but I seem to stop and start a lot, then lose momentum. What am I doing wrong?

You now know to first assess if your goal is too big. The second possibility is that it is too vague. You feel like you are ready, but you really aren't sure where to begin or what step is next. Untangle this obstacle by asking lots of questions like:

- How am I going to do this?
- When do I want it done?
- What equipment, education, help, might I need to begin?

The more questions you ask, and the more concrete answers you gather, the more truly Ready you will be. If you couple that practice with a good dose of commitment, you'll be primed for success.

You may still feel like you have lots of questions about your Readiness. I'm going to ask you to boldly forge on. As, I believe all the answers will be provided as you move through the book.

Readiness: Great Ways to Break It Down

Not clear on the whole readiness thing? Don't want to know right now how ready you are? No worries! Here's a great way to break down Readiness into smaller practices that will move you closer to becoming ready.

1. Practice honesty. (Yikes! Scary, I know.) Pause and ask, "Do I really want to make time to do this now?"

2. Start a list of actionable tasks you *could* do when you are ready. No obsessing here. This is a 15 - 30 second "job." Add no more than one task per day. Actionable tasks begin with words like: write, call, measure, visit, review, etc.

3. If the answer is, "I'm not ready to take action on a task or goal." practice putting it mentally on hold, allowing yourself to put it aside, devoting no energy to it, until you *are* ready.
   Note: Practice congratulating yourself for being self-aware.

4. Practice being aware of projects that continually surface on your mental To-Do list but never get any of your energy. Just observe how frequently you do this.

5. If it feels right, take the previous practice of putting items on mental hold one step further. When the thoughts of the task arise, remind yourself that you have put this on the back burner... then add a time limit to revisit i.e. 3 months from now, in May, etc. Now, you don't have to think about it at all until the revisit date.
   Note: This task will continue to mentally resurface. Gently

remind yourself that you've put it on hold and that's good, very good. Celebrate your success. You are learning to let things go.

6. Practice: When an idea/goal pops into your mind practice asking "Why do I want this?" Expect more from yourself than "It will make me happy." Go deeper. Explore why you are, or are not ready at this time. Just observe your answer.

Reflections on Readiness

What worries came up? What choices can you make to improve your Readiness?

_____

_____

What words, phrases or whole sentences did you hear in your mind while reading about readiness?

_____

_____

Are you experiencing anxiety or frustration in reference to Readiness? To keep your life manageable, yet begin to move toward your goal, what Great Ways to Break It Down activity will you commit to as you begin this journey?

_____

_____

Write one positive comment about yourself and your goal setting abilities. If you get stuck you can try: I prepare for new goals by…

_____

_____

What, if any, Ah-ha observations did you have about Readiness?

_____

_____

Changing your mindset with an affirmation:

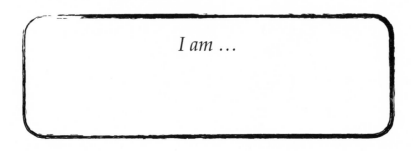

I am ...

Need a suggestion?

I prepare for new activities with honesty and clarity.

To recap where you are in the process you have: 1) stated your goal, 2) explored Your Big Why, and 3) assessed your Readiness. Now it's time for step 4), refining your goal with clarity and purpose.

Mapping Your Goal
Step 4 Refining Your Goal

Visual Goal Mapping™ is a goal setting system which frees you from all the "what if's" and "I can't's." It allows you to see all the parts of your goal, your strengths and struggles; it identifies roadblocks and naturally breaks goals down into manageable tasks.

Here's what you need to create your Visual Goal Map:

Materials List

☑ 1 standard folder, no pockets (I like pretty colored ones, but plain manila will work also)

☑ 1 pad 2" x 2", or smaller, sticky notes. (do not use the bigger, standard size)

☑ Pen

The Magic Begins Here

Rewrite your three goals from The Big Why exercise.

Goal 1

_____

_____

_____

Goal 2

_____

_____

_____

Goal 3

_____

_____

_____

*Please note, from here we will be dividing your big goal into smaller tasks.

Coaches Comment:
Be kind. This is a new skill you are practicing. You are not committed to anything this time around except learning the process.

Mapping Your Goal

1. Think about each of these goals and decide which one is most interesting to work on or most interesting to you. Note: please choose a challenging goal that may cause some worry, confusion or feels vague. You are using this goal as a sample to learn Visual Goal Mapping. There is no commitment to follow through at this time.

   If, for some reason, you want to chose a different goal from the one you used in the Big Why exercise, that's OK. You will, however, need to redo The Big Why worksheet for this new goal.

2. Write the goal you have chosen for this exercise in large letters across the inside top of your folder, and on the tab. It will look like this:

3. Thought Clearing - Using one Post It stickie note per thought, emotion, idea or task, write down anything and everything that comes to mind associated with this goal. Stick each note to the

inside of your folder. Let it flow. Clear your mind of all thoughts related to this goal. Don't worry about punctuation, capitalization, correct spelling or complete sentences. Don't worry if the thought makes sense or where you place the stickie. Just get it all out.

Example:
Goal ~ Paint the Kitchen.

Tasks / thoughts / emotions might be:
- ☐ choose paint color
- ☐ measure how big room is
- ☐ I hate to paint
- ☐ hire painter
- ☐ Sam, my partner, is going to be difficult
- ☐ overwhelmed
- ☐ worried

You will probably have lots more stickies than this. They will look something like this:

Coaches Comment:

Generally, if a stickie requires several steps, as in the case of Hire a painter, I recommend breaking it down even further. When broken down this stickie might become: 1) Call friends and ask for referrals. 2) Look on Angie's List for a painter with a good rating. 3) Narrow recommendations down to top three. 4) Contact selected painters. 5) Choose painter.

This may seem a bit tedious, or over zealous at first, but, imagine how much better it would feel to have five small successes verses five places to: get distracted, forget, reschedule, lose a phone number, or countless other "failures."

With bigger tasks, by the time you actually hire the painter, you are exhausted. You are so relieved to have someone...anyone, coming to paint your room it doesn't occur to you that you've actually completed a big job!

By breaking tasks down into micro manageable activities you come to appreciate how many steps it actually takes to complete a seemingly simple task. You also open up dozens of golden opportunities to feel successful. Each time one of these perfect gems is scheduled and completed you get an Atta Girl!

Troubleshooting Stickie Notes (Round 1) :

How can someone have trouble with their stickies, you ask? Easy… and, it happens all the time. We are all so used to filtering and blocking thoughts, that some just never make it onto a stickie. Frequently, it's the lost thoughts and emotions that may be the most important to capture.

 Emotions…nope, I don't have any stickies like that. Why would I?

Jon was a numbers guy, very analytical. His goal was to take his insurance business to the next level, which included hiring new team members, upping his game with cold calls, presentations, and other business building tasks. He was in his twenties and came from a long line of insurance brokers. He expressed pride in his lineage and wanted to make his dad and granddad proud.

Jon's detail oriented mind loved the stickie exercise. He loved thinking of all the tasks he already new he needed to put into place for success.

When we got to the step of sorting the stickies (more about sorting in the next section), Jon had no emotional responses, no random thoughts. Just tasks.

At first, you may think, "That's great, I wish I thought that clearly." And you'd be right up to a point. It is a gift to be able to clearly break down a project. However, it is also essential to listen for the voice in your head that may be undermining your progress, or creating hidden obstacles. Trust me, it's there.

I asked Jon to sit with the goal for a few minutes and imagine all that it was going to take to put this into action. After some quiet time, he started writing more stickies. He wrote, "overwhelming," "not sure I'm good enough yet," and "pressure."

Then, we went one step deeper. I asked him to think about his father and grandfather, their success and experience, and what he feels about being a part of the family business. I also asked him to observe if there were sensations in his body associated with this topic, and if there were, where he was experiencing them.

After an even longer pause, he put his hand on his stomach. His breathing became slightly more rapid. He picked up his pen and wrote "fear of failure," "fear of disappointing them." Then, he put the pen down and sighed. There was a completeness to the new silence, as though all that needed to be said had been.

I asked Jon to describe what was different now.

He replied, "I didn't want to think about, and especially voice my fears and concerns. I've always been told to focus on the positive. But, I noticed when I was holding my fears in, there was a stiffness to my body, especially in my stomach. Now that I've written my fears down, they don't seem so big, and my stomach has relaxed."

He continued, "My Dad and Grandpa would never feel disappointment if I didn't reach these new goals. They are my biggest supporters. They'd just ask if I needed help."

This scenario frequently happens with people who are analytical, linear thinkers, those with a "Just do it!" attitude, or those who were taught to "suck it up."

This is a wonderful skill to be blessed with; *AND*, it can be an obstacle. Hidden, unvoiced fears hold us back in ways we can't imagine.

If no, or very few emotions show up in your stickies, create some quiet time (at least 15 minutes) to sit with this project and allow yourself to think about all the tasks. What does it feel like to bring the whole project into your mind at once? Where in your body are you experiencing sensations? What are you feeling? Tension? Pain? Shaking? Excitement? You may find that it is suddenly terrifying. Whatever you are experiencing is OK.

Now that you know that the idea of this project is enormous, and that there are emotions and fears associated with it, you will need to proceed with some caution and care. You will need to break it down to *really* small tasks to keep it manageable, and be continually aware of any emotions that arise.

 I don't understand, none of my stickies seem like tasks. There's nothing to actually do. How do I proceed?

Some of us deal with life's tasks and situations through the filters of emotion and sensation. Most "creatives" fall into this category. If this is you, your first response to an experience tends to be defined by feelings. You may find yourself actually using the phrase "I feel..." a lot.

Visual Goal Mapping is so perfect for you it makes me want to dance! Much like Jon's ability to see the details in the story above, your sensitivity is a gift, provided you have tools to deconstruct those feelings into tasks.

Sonya was a highly creative doula, passionate about helping new, pregnant moms have a beautiful birthing experience. She was kindness personified. Her goal was to create a business of heart-centered doulas and other holistic pre-natal practitioners.

When we started the stickie exercise, Sonya's hand couldn't write fast enough. She had 20 stickies in a matter of moments. When we got to the sorting practice, she looked completely lost and confused.

This is why I love this exercise! Sonya's stickies said things like:

- Feels right
- Finally doing this
- Do I want an office?
- Too much to do
- Who will I get to work with me?
- What services should I offer?

There is nothing wrong with Sonya's stickies. This is the way she thinks. That being said, they are a mix of emotional responses, sensations and questions. There were no actionable tasks, meaning there were no stickies with words like: hire, write, organize, call, etc.

Therefore, Sonya is generally going to have trouble knowing where to begin. She needs to learn to translate her sensations and feelings into actions.

To begin this translation process with Sonya, I asked her to reexamine the stickies that she had worded as questions.

For example, the stickie that read "Do I want an office?" we changed to "*Decide* if I want an office." Decide is a verb and therefore an action that Sonya could "Do."

As she was writing new stickie, and thought about it further, she began discussing the pros and cons for office space versus home office. In that moment, she decided the pros for office space far outweighed the cons.

With that clarity, the new and final stickie read "Locate office space." That was something Sonya could do, "Locate." It was an action.

The biggest challenge for you emotional, "sensation-al" thinkers is that all of these feelings float around and around in your head as though they are tasks. But, by their very nature, they ask you to feel more, but take no action. Your brain will continue to spin, looking for something to do.

Once you write it down and translate it into an actionable task, your brain will find a solution and let it go. Until that point, you are just rehashing feelings, which can be highly stressful. I have created a list of descriptive words to help you translate your feelings into tasks. The list is called Action Words To Clarify Tasks and Goals. You'll find the list in the Index Section. Check it out! It will make your goal setting lists much more effective.

If this sounds like you, there will be more tools later in this section to help you begin to create actionable stickies.

The important thing to remember for now is to allow yourself to do the Thought Clearing exercise without the restriction of translating. Let the emotions and sensations flow freely. Once they are out you can teach your executive brain to sort and translate. With time, it will happen more naturally and with less effort.

Visual Goal Mapping™ allows you to see your obstacles without judgement. The self-knowledge you can gain from this process can be profound. You will begin to develop an objective view of how your brain works, lays things out. Knowing how your brain works is a huge step in gaining control of your life, time and schedule.

Coaches Comment:
Once again, this is a new skill you are just learning. You can't get it wrong. You can only try. If you have learned something about yourself celebrate this new insight.

Reflections on Stickies and Mapping So Far

Take a moment to reflect on your stickies and jot down any additional thoughts, concerns, or"ah-ha's" you want to remember. Don't overthink it. Be open to the flow.

Frequently, when we are learning something new, old stories, thoughts or frustrations can come up and get in the way of our progress. What thoughts did you have while going through this section?

_____

_____

_____

If they were negative, can you attempt to view them as old stories, beliefs you hold that no longer serve you? What positive action can you take right now to be open to learning this new material?

_____

_____

_____

 ## A Brief Detour into SMART Goals

It's impossible to go any further without talking about SMART goals. Designed to put clear, defining parameters on goals to assure success, this acronym should be referenced when setting all of your tasks and goals until it become second nature.

The concept of SMART goals was first coined in 1981 in Peter Drucker's *Management by Objectives*. The primary advantage of applying the SMART acronym to goal setting is that it makes goals easier to understand, outline and execute.

The SMART goals concept is widely used in the business world where it is primarily applied to project management and professional development. Outside the business world, it can be applied to anything that has tasks and objectives, from weight loss, to painting your living room, to a change in careers.

SMART stands for...

Specific: Your goal needs to have as many details as possible. Using question words as prompts will help you flesh out this step.

Example:
- Who can I ask for help?
- How big, small, costly, etc.?
- What do I want the end result to be?
- Where am I going to do this?
- Save the "when" question for the "T" part of SMART.

Remember Sonya, our sensitive entrepreneur with an abundance of stickies? The "S" in the SMART goal process is an essential step for emotional processors and "creatives. "This is where the translation happens. Be vigilant with this step. Turn feelings into actions here with question and by making them…

 Measurable: Asks how will you measure success or completion. You can measure in dollars saved or earned, clients gained, distance traveled, hours of engagement, or any other unit of measure that applies to your goal. You can see from this definition why "I want to be happier." isn't a SMART goal. How would you measure milestones, or success? When are you done?

There's one more really important clarification. In order to be a smart (Punny, right?) and SMART goal, the way you measure must match what you are measuring.

I worked with a client once who told me her goal was to lose weight. When I asked what she currently weighed, she replied, "I don't know. I refuse to step on a scale."

Although I understood where she was coming from, I explained that if she refused to get on a scale, her goal could not be "to lose weight." We needed to change the goal to fit a tool of measurement that worked for her.

First, we discussed several tools of measuring success aimed at her desire to become a thinner person like:

• Being able to walk X number of miles per day by…

- Consistently eating X number of calories per day
- A Change in dress size.

Any of these, with clear parameters, would have produced the desired result. She finally chose to use dress size as her mile marker and measuring tool of success.

We changed her goal from "I want to lose weight" to "I want to be smaller around." Perfect! We could set mile markers for success based on dress size, for example: down one dress size by eight weeks, two sizes in four months, etc. Most important, she would know when to celebrate success. Now the tool to measure (dress size) matched the goal (getting smaller).

SMART Goal Check In
If, after using the Measurable criteria you are unable to match tools to milestones / markers re-visit and re-word your stickies assuring they describe actual tasks. In other words, get more Specific.

 Achievable or Assignable: Achievable asks you to consider your readiness to achieve this goal in your current situation. If, upon close scrutiny, the answer is "no, it's not achievable under my current conditions," it doesn't mean you give up on the goal. It simply raises awareness of the influences, skills and readiness of your life in this moment and allows for planning.

Example:

You want to launch a new product line. You estimate it will take an extra 15 hours/week for the next six months to develop the recipe, decide on packaging, create a marketing campaign, and put it into production.

Is this Achievable? You recently lost one of your best employees. You already work a 50 hour week. To make up for the loss of this valuable employee, you will have to put in a minimum of five extra hours/week to cover the shortage of help, find time to advertise for a new employee, and then interview and train them.

Light bulb moment! You do not have time right now to take on this new project because your business is currently understaffed. Your new product development and launch will have to wait at least 3 months.

You give yourself permission to set this new project aside (not devoting any more mental energy to it) and revisit the new product launch at the end of three months.

You celebrate your good judgement and planning. Consequently, you sleep well tonight. You are amazing!

Assignable is sometimes used in place of **Achievable**. I prefer Assignable for the "A" since Achievable and Realistic are so similar. You won't lose anything by making this switch. Also, Assignable reminds you to look outside yourself when planning. It raises questions like

- Where do I need help?
- Who can help me with tasks I'm not good at?

- Who (in the organization, group, family) handles this type of task?

Example:
You are launching a new business as a bookkeeper. Numbers make your heart sing! You understand and love the details of setting up all the books for a new business. One of your goals is to have a warm, but classy office to reassure high paying clients that you have the know how and you mean business.

Although a "numbers wonder woman," you can't seem to get dressed in the morning. You notice your pants are rumpled and hope it doesn't matter. And, shoot... did you really manage to put on two different shoes? Oh, well. You know numbers and that's what counts. Right?

Wrong. If your goal is to have a classy, warm office and you have little interest or ability to put your clothes together, then you need help. One of your assignable tasks must be "Consult a decorator."

For the purposes of better understanding, suppose your original stickie said "hire a decorator." This is where the translation phase becomes very important and can help overcome obstacles.

All too frequently the word "hire" immediately means money you don't have. Consequently, a mental door closes. "I don't have money, therefore I can't even consider..." What about translating the word hire to "consult?" Does that have a different feel? "Consult" just reminds you to have a conversation with someone. The financial obstacle is removed. Translation here is essential especially when it comes to money.

Back to our example. Because you are now just looking to innocently consult someone, your brain is no longer frozen in "I can't" mode. Your unblocked brain helpfully reminds you of Paul, a man you just met who has a new decorating business. You two really hit if off. Maybe Paul would be open to a barter: you do his books; he decorates your office. Win-Win!

Paul loves the idea! You successfully launch your business and clients are impressed with your new space and your credentials. They happily hand over their books and joyfully write you a big check! You are a superstar! You celebrate your success with an ice cream sundae. Well done, you!

 Realistic: To me, Realistic was included to make a clever acronym as it covers the same territory as achievable. That being said, there are times that a reality check is called for.

I did a workshop once, where a participant had four big goals for the next two years: 1) get a masters degree, 2) run for county council, 3) start a family and 4) have more quality time with her husband.

Although there was some initial resistance to accept the obvious, after very little discussion, and implementing the SMART goal exercise, she realized that this picture was just not Realistic, no matter how much she wanted it to be.

At least two of these goals probably needed to go on the back burner for a while, as they were mutually exclusive. You can't go back to

school while working full time, adding more time away from home, *and* have more time with your husband.

Why does this matter? Shouldn't people have goals, or dreams? Goals and dreams are what makes the world go around. However, when you continually hold a long, useless list of them in your head it can become very disheartening, especially if they are unrealistic. You can begin to think you're lazy, unfocused, or worse.

I can't tell you the number of women I have worked with who publish books, take care of ailing, live-in parents, actively participant in their communities, and work a full 40 plus hour work week. Because their expectations of themselves are unrealistic, these Wonder Women surprisingly refer to themselves as lazy because they haven't completed some goal on their list. They are not, by any definition of the word, lazy.

To restate, and this is important, *what they are* is unrealistic in their expectations of their time and abilities.

When you take the time to lay out your goals, review them using the iSMART concepts, then you can see... really see, where there are conflicting objectives, it becomes clear where you have been holding onto goals that no longer serve your purpose, lifestyle or calendar. And... you can let them go!

Holding that list of unrealistic goals in your head takes up the valuable brain energy and space you need for your Game Changer goals, the goals that are going to change your life. This is why the "R" in SMART is extremely important.

You want to be devoting your valuable time and mental energy to your Game Changers. Being Realistic is what will bring your Game Changers to the top of your list. Completing these goals will give you a feeling of success, the ability to say "I rock!" Trust me, you do!

 Time Table: Asks you to place a completion date or time on your goal.

Estimating how long a task takes can be a big obstacle. Those who chronically underestimate time become frustrated because they expect to complete the task and don't, which can be a tremendous disappointment. Or, they underestimate time and now find they don't have the energy to see the task through to completion. Either way, underestimating time can be a real challenge.

Learning how long it takes *you* to do something is an essential part of successful goal completion. Understanding your speed and focus for different types of work will take some trial and error. But, it can be learned. Don't skip this step. It is an important part of the process. Hang in there!

This is a great place for a reminder to make each of these processes your own. While writing this book, I came to realize that creating a Time Table makes me anxious. I am a very hard worker, totally a Type A overachiever. I'm also a person recovering from some serious health issues that require me to be very mindful of my energy expenditure. When I am able to work, I work really hard; yet, I can still forget to stop and rest. (I'm a work in progress.)

Having a predefined deadline did not work for me in writing this book. Health issues wrecked my deadline plans. So, I changed to a more realistic goals like: "I will work on it when my health allows.""I will just keep showing up." These goals may sound vague, but they worked for me because I know myself. I never give up on something I really want.

The result? No anxiety and a completed book. For me, "When I can" became my Time Table. The point? Observe yourself carefully. Make the practice your own.

OOPS! We're not quite done. That's SMART with an 'I'.

 Innovation: The word Innovation is sometimes added to the SMART goals model (maybe iSMART, like iPhone to help you remember).

New research has found that in corporate settings, fostering innovation and creativity keeps projects and programs vibrant. Projects and programs are the corporate equivalent of goals. By including Innovation in the SMART goal mix, flexibility and "out of the box" thinking happen. Bottom line, be flexible when looking for solutions. Innovation and creativity provide a rich groundwork for new opportunities and outcomes.

Coaches Comment:
This is the perfect moment for a coaching check-in. There is no expectation that you are going to do all of this your first time through and exactly as it is described. Make this work for you by focusing on just one of the SMART goal objectives for the next few weeks. There is an enormous amount of great information here. What one topic really interests you right now? How can you make it work for you?

Now that we've discussed iSMART goals, you are ready to continue with your goal and to continue clarifying and mapping your stickies. To review, you have:

- Created three goals
- Identified one goal you are going to work on
- Completed the Thought Clearing exercise to empty your mind of all associated thoughts and tasks

Now it's time to apply some iSMARTs to your stickie tasks.

NEXT

Back to Mapping

As a reminder, in our mapping exercise, so far you have stated your goal and done the Thought Clearing Exercise. Now onto Step 4, sorting.

4. Sort and clarify your stickies. With objective eyes, and a focus on your goal, select all the *actionable* tasks, stickies that have words like: Get, Take, Plan, Talk to, Make, Go to, and put them on one side of the folder. If you are struggling to think of action words, refer to the Action Words List in the Nitty Gritty (reference) Section (Don't be afraid to add new tasks or emotions if they arise.)

Example:
The initial list for the goal of painting the kitchen was:
- ☐ choose paint color
- ☐ measure how big room is
- ☐ I hate to paint
- ☐ hire painter
- ☐ Sam, my partner, is going to be difficult
- ☐ overwhelmed
- ☐ worried

Two of these five stickie tasks do not contain an action (aside from the two purely emotional stickies, overwhelmed and worried) and might get in the way of moving forward. See if you can figure out which ones they are?

If you selected I hate to paint, and Sam is going to be difficult, you were right. Neither of these describe an action that can be taken to move closer to the goal of painting the room. They need to be translated

Coaches Comment:
If your stickie does not contain an action word, it might need to be translated into an action, otherwise it might become an obstacle.

If you are finding translating a struggle refer to the Action Words to Clarify Tasks and Goals List in the Nitty Gritty (reference) Section of this book. You can also use measurement or completion dates to turn a vague stickie task into actionable steps, which translates into success!

I hate to paint can be translated into:

☐ Brainstorm ways to make painting fun. (Action: brainstorm)
☐ Create small milestones and corresponding rewards that make painting fun. (Action: create)

Milestone: Paint wall #1 by Saturday night. **Reward**: Take a bath using fancy bath bomb and special soap while enjoying my favorite hot tea. (measurement/milestone: paint wall #1, completion date Saturday night)

Let's look at another one…
Sam is going to be difficult can be translated to:
☐ Talk with Sam about ways to make this enjoyable by Tuesday. (Action: talk to) OR,
☐ Invite Sam to visit his Mom while painting is taking place. (Action: invite)

Do you see the difference? Brainstorm, talk, create and invite are all tasks you can schedule and check off when they are done. That's how you move from a murky To-Do list to one with clarity and purpose.

Let's continue to bring even more clarity to your goal. You've translated the non-actionable goals. Now, examine any remaining tasks to assure they are as clear and actionable as possible.

If you remember, for the purposes of our working example, the action based tasks are:

• *hire* painter
• *measure* room
• *choose* paint color

If you feel confident these are clear and essential tasks for getting a room painted you are ready to move on.

Finally, move all the feelings-based, or random thought stickies onto the back of your folder, out of sight. Your feelings can frequently be the obstacles that get in your way. By simply calling them out, you can more easily figure out how to move past them. You will find more about feelings-based stickies in the Troubleshooting Stickies pages at the end of the section.

As a reminder, the feelings based stickies are:

- overwhelmed
- worried
- I hate to paint, may also qualify.

When you are done with all of your translating, sorting and moving, your folder will now look something like this:

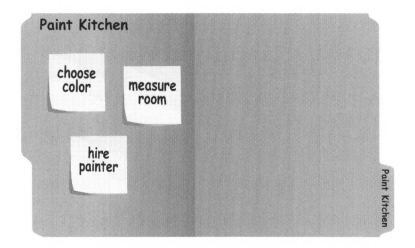

5. Arrange tasks in the order in which they need to be done. For example, in the case of painting your kitchen, "measure room" or "choose color" would probably be first. Sometimes, as with this example, the order may not be tremendously important.

However, both of these tasks need to come before "buy paint" for obvious reasons

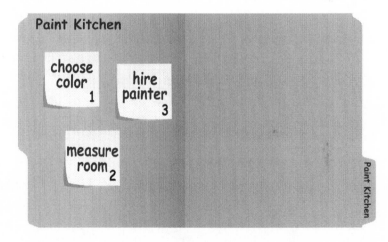

If you have a large number of stickies this step may be a bit challenging and require some trial and error. Be patient and kind.

6. Using a pencil, write the order of each task in the bottom right corner. Your sticky notes now look like this:

7. Estimate how long each task will take to complete. If you are chronically late or always running out of
time, then over-estimate the time each task will take. This is a great lesson in your perceptions versus reality.

When the time comes to execute your tasks, be open to the process, meaning, don't expect your estimating to be perfect the first time.

If you don't complete a task in the given time, it doesn't mean you are a failure or never going to get it right. It just means you are in the learning stage. Keep padding your estimating until you come up with something that seems to be accurate.

For example: "hmmm… even after adding an extra 15 minutes to each of my tasks I still ran out of time. From now on, I need to give myself an extra 30 minutes for this type of task.
This is really valuable information if you choose to learn from it. Train your brain. You've got this!

Coaches Comment

Estimating Time: Much like putting your tasks in order, the time a task will take can be another stumbling block, creating feelings of frustration, confusion and failure. Step 7 is a practice that will help you better understand if you are an under-estimator. Leave the guilt and judgement of past behaviors behind. Be kind and allow yourself the opportunity to learn a new and valuable tool. Celebrate your new awareness… awareness is success!

8. Now, write the estimated time on the bottom left corner of the stickie note. Remember, *this is still an estimate.* Don't worry if you don't get it right. As mentioned in step 7, you will get better with practice.

Example:

You estimate painting your kitchen, start to finish, is going to take you eight hours. You can't stand painting and have no tolerance or attention span for this type of work. The obvious choice is to hire someone, but you suddenly realize you can't afford it. If it's going to get painted, you have to do it. You have several options:

A. You decide that realistically, you can manage two hours at a time. You block off four, two hour blocks over the next few days or weeks and get it done. You celebrate your success!

B. You recognize the conundrum you are in and get creative. You invite three friends to a Paint & Pizza Party. You provide the food and binge watch Game of Thrones while painting. You all have a blast! The room gets painted and you are crowned the Paint Party Genius! Your friends copy this great idea and get their rooms painted, as well. They give you a special Paint Party Genius T Shirt to celebrate your brilliance!

Back to your stickies

Paint party or painter...you have put your stickies in order and have estimated the time it will take for each task. Your stickies will now look like this:

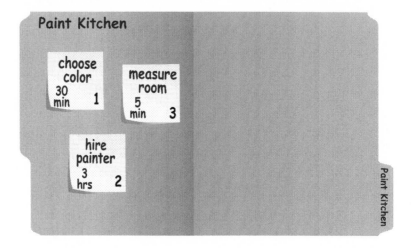

The whole point of steps 7 & 8 is to find out where you do and don't estimate time well and plan accordingly. If it's a task you do somewhat frequently, i.e. cleaning the house, bookkeeping, making a certain number of phone calls, I suggest tracking the time and writing it down.

From this directory of observations, you can begin to create an easy reference of the "Time it Takes Me To..." activities. After you refer to it a couple of times, memory will kick in and you won't have to look again. Feel free to add to this directory as new, repeating tasks present themselves. Over time, you will get very good at estimating how much time it takes you to get things done

SMART Goal Check In

It is important, at this point, to add up all the time it will take to complete this goal and ask yourself "Do I have time in my calendar for this goal?" If the answer is a resounding "yes!" Excellent! You are ready to schedule.

If your answer is "Wow! That's going to take a lot more time than I thought! But, I still really want to do this now." The next question you need to ask is, "How is this going to fit in my current schedule?"

Congratulations! You have just learned a valuable Time Table skill! You are going to have to do a little, or a lot of prioritizing (see Prioritizing Chapter) to make this goal a reality. Visual Goal Mapping is your road map to success.

However, if your answer is "Holy hamburgers! There's no way I can do this now." Congratulations! You have just learned how to manage your calendar by being Realistic. Don't despair. Your goal is not lost forever. Keep reading and you will find out how to save your mapped goal for the future, when you do have the time.

There's a lot of new information in this section. Please remember, you can always…

Brief Reflections on Estimating Time

I've added a brief reflection time here because estimating time seems to be challenging for a lot of people. It may help to take a moment to pause and think on any additional thoughts, concerns, or "ah-ha's" that came up for you in steps 7 & 8, or your relationship with time, in general.

What, if any, emotions do you experience when thinking about time? Pause and observe any sensations in your body.

_____

_____

What thoughts are going through your mind as you think about estimating time? Pause and listen to any words or phrases that are being voiced in your head.

_____

_____

Do you have any concerns about your ability to deal with time in a more effective manner? Why or why not?

_____

_____

Congratulations!
You are now ready to make a commitment to this goal. Let's get this goal scheduled.

Troubleshooting Your Stickies (Round 2)

 Help! I have a million stickies!

There is nothing wrong with having a lot of stickies. In fact, it is a great teaching tool. First, you now know why it may be a real challenge for you to get anything done. You've been holding all this stuff in your head, taking up valuable memory/brain space.

Now that all of these thoughts are out of your head you can: take vague stickies and make them more specific, toss out stickies that are not task-oriented, target problems or issues you've identified and seek solutions. Celebrate the fact that you now have a way to clear your mind!

 One of my stickies is going to take a really long time to complete...definitely more than a day. Do I do something special or different with this stickie?

For tasks that are going to take long periods of time, break them down into smaller units or tasks. (Let's agree that "long" is subjective, but definitely more than one day.) Painting a room is an example of a goal that could take more than eight hours. If it's going to take several days or longer, this actually requires a folder of it's own.

For example, it's a frequent occurrence for me to see people using one stickie for "create my website." Creating a website, whether you are doing it yourself or hiring someone, takes a lot of thought, planning and work. In this case, start a new goal folder called Create

My Website, and begin the stickie process all over again. There can be many dozens of tasks associated with creating a new website.

One stickie with "Create a website" is the equivalent of a stickie that reads "End world hunger." It's never, NEVER going to be accomplished with a single action or stickie.

 I'm still struggling with the order of tasks. For some reason I just can't imagine the sequence of events. Is there any help for me?

If you get bogged down or side tracked easily because you don't know what comes next, try working backward. Imagine the project is complete. Keeping the image of the completed project in your mind, (for clarity what you've written on the folder tab is your goal) ask yourself, "What came before...?"

Example:
Let's go back to the example of painting a room. Imagine you have just plopped down on your couch, exhausted from a job well done. The room is finished and it's beautiful.

☑ What did you do before you allowed yourself the luxury of admiring your handiwork? You put the furniture back in its place.

☑ What came before you put the furniture back? You cleaned up all the drop clothes, paint brushes, paint cans and masking tape.

☑ What did you do before the trash clean up?

You get the idea.

I'm not into all that touchy-feely stuff. Whining doesn't do anyone any good. My philosophy is to push through and get it done. Do I have to "sit with" my goal and try feeling something?

The short answer is, "no." No one can make you do anything. And, I wouldn't dream of trying. That being said, I will add that you can't conquer what you refuse to name.

During a workshop I hosted, there was a "Just Do It" kind of gal. Through the morning's group exchanges, it became obvious she was quite fearless in many areas of her life. When we talked about stepping outside your comfort zone she proudly stated, "What do you write if don't fear anything?"

When I asked her to read her stickies, she had no emotional, feeling stickies. I commented on that and asked her to close her eyes and imagine making herself vulnerable, to open herself up to the idea of being afraid.

"No way!" she said.

"Dip your toe in it." I suggested. "You can peek at that place. You don't have to stay there. You just might learn something really important."

If you are afraid to even explore the idea of your fear, you have no way of planning how to combat it. In the end, it will show up in unknown, frequently unseen ways: headaches, sore throats, frequent colds, unexplained tiredness, irritability. These are just some of the ways your body deals with avoided emotions.

You can use a lot of energy stuffing that junk down, refusing to acknowledge that it exists. Imagine if all that great powerful energy was being used in a positive way, to face your fears and finally put them behind you? Wouldn't that be an amazing goal to have accomplished? Absolutely! It could be life changing

 .Ugh! I've really tried. I just can't figure out how to make this stickie task measurable.

You are not alone. This skill can be challenging. The benefit is you have just discovered an area that requires a little attention for you to complete your goals.

Begin with looking at the verbs (action words) you are using. Stickies that have verbs like: feel, be and want, do not describe how the task is going to be accomplished.

Call, run, write, jump, measure, research, are all words that call for action and define how the task gets done. Go back to your vague, non-action stickies and try applying these types of words.

Be Happier

I can't tell you the number of times I see stickies that say "be happier," "feel better," or "healthier." The question has to be asked. How? How are you going to know when you are done? When are you happier? Let's use "Be happier" as an example of the questions you might ask to clarify the required actions.

Sample Questions:
- How will I know when I have reached "happier?"
- When I envision myself as finally happy, what am I doing?
- What does my life look like?
- How am I behaving?

Create new stickies with the answers to these questions. Example:

Question: What makes me happy?
Thought: Reading makes me happy.
New Stickie: Make time to read two times/week
Measurement: Two times/week

Question: How will I know when I am happier?
Thought: I will be patient with my kids for three days in a row.
New Stickie: Three times a day, when I feel impatient with my kids, or anyone, I will pause and take a breath.
Measurement: Three times a day.

You get the idea.

Coaches Comment:
During the Thought Clearing exercise try not to censure your thoughts by attempting to write the perfect stickies on the first try. The whole point of the Thought Clearing is to get everything out of your head without getting bogged down in the process of how it will happen. Clarifying and sorting always takes place after the Clearing.

This stickie is too hard. How do I actually make any headway?

Give this book to a friend. Curl up in a ball. Binge eat chocolate and cake! Only kidding. You've got this.

> **Any time a stickie feels too big, *break it down.***

This question is really common. Feel free to replace "hard" with overwhelming, expensive, time consuming… or any other word that might come after the word "too." Being more specific with exactly what part of this is too much, or what exact emotion this is evoking will help you move closer to a solution.

Any stickie that feels "too" anything needs to be broken down. Sometimes the stickie is so big it needs its own folder, as in Make my website.

Other times, it may require clear time parameters to make it manageable, as with the case of the eight hour painting job (broken into four, two hour sessions).

Or, if it's still "too" something, it may require a little brainstorming to figure out what smaller actions are required. Then, create a list (or more stickies) detailing each smaller action in the new process.

Finally, go back to step 6 and put these new tasks in order. By coming up with really simple, small tasks you can derail emotional responses.

For example, imagine your stickie is to call the IRS and get a tax question answered. For whatever reason, this feels too big. You know it's going to take *F O R E V E R* because your friend just did this and was on the phone for *H O U R S*.

Second, you're positive that whatever they need, you are not going to have, which will require a second, third... who knows how many more phone calls. You don't have this kind of time. Period!

Let's take a moment and deconstruct this.

1. "This is going to take forever" is an emotional response, a fear (in this case a fear of wasted time). It may, or may not take a long time. If the call has to be made for you to move forward, be smart and plan accordingly. Use the On Hold time to listen to calming music and work on a task like check writing. Your time is no longer wasted. You are an awesome time management maven!

2. "Whatever they need I won't have." This is also an emotional response of fear (fear of being unprepared and losing valuable time). Sadly, there are some tasks that have an amount of uncertainty built into them. The motor vehicle department and IRS happen to fall into this category. You can fight it, try to avoid it, be angry about it, or accept it as a given. It really doesn't matter which option you choose. It's going to require what it requires. Again, plan accordingly.

   Here's where breaking it down comes in very handy. Let's replay this whole scenario using the idea of breaking it down.

   Stickie: Call the IRS

Breaking it down into tasks:

☐ Find the number for the IRS.
  Time required: 30 seconds
☐ Research online information and documents needed from an IRS advisor to answer my question.
  Time required: 20 minutes
☐ Create list of tasks I can do while on hold.
  Time required: five minutes
☐ Schedule two hour block for IRS call.
  Time required: 30 seconds
☐ Schedule one hour time block to collect needed documents and information for follow up phone call, including tasks to do while on hold.
  Time required: 15 minutes.

> **You don't have to see the whole staircase, just take the first step.**
> Martin Luther King

Here's the beauty of this plan. First, you can begin this task without picking up the phone and wasting a frightening amount of time on hold. You can boldly and proactively move forward without any of your fears getting in your way. There are no unknown time sucks, no surprises. Several of these steps require just a few minutes of prep. Check that box as done!

Second, no matter what happens, the time is not wasted because you have planned to use the hold time wisely.

Third, there is no room or reason for feelings of frustration and anger. There are no unknowns. No one is going to take you or your time for granted. You are completely in charge of the whole situation.

Fourth, when broken down this way, you get to keep checking off the boxes when completed, experiencing that overwhelming sense of joy that comes with knowing you are moving forward, no matter how small the job.

And, finally. It may not take two hours or a second phone call.

Huzzah! You just gained several hours in your schedule. Take time to celebrate how clever and organized you are! Win-win!

Those fearful stickies are still scaring me.

I'm not suggesting that your fears are not legitimate or still frightening. However, what I do know is that the fear comes from thinking of the task in its entirety. Take the example of public speaking, a huge fear for most of the population. If your stickie is "schedule one speaking gig" and you are terrified of public speaking, there's no amount of stickie magic that will make that fear go away.

For you, this task is too big and will require you to break it down into very tiny tasks like: research a topic, find places to speak, research anxiety around public speaking, hire someone to work with me on my public speaking, pick three new tools to overcome my anxiety and practice them. You see? All of these activities will result with you killing it in front of a crowd!

The point is you are not afraid of research, reading about anxiety, thinking of a topic. All of these small, fearless tasks get a check mark next to them when completed and require no courage. Because, you are not speaking... yet.

Ultimately, you will get to the place that you have to speak. But, I guarantee it will be a lot easier and less stressful than it would have been if it just remained on your list as "schedule a speaking gig." And, think of how good you will feel knowing you are always moving closer and closer to conquering that fear!! You get to be a Super Power Woman!

For some, this stickie practice can be overwhelming, at first, if you let it. Please do not get bogged down with the entire process. Choose one part of the whole exercise that provided the most Ah-Ha moments and make that your customized practice, meaning, figure out how to make it manageable for you.

For example, for the next month set aside three 5 minute sessions to do the Thought Clearing exercise, to clear your brain. That's it. Once that feels comfortable, you can add putting tasks in order, or just estimating time for certain activities.

Once you do each part, or the whole exercise a couple of times, you will see your strengths and struggles and be able to use Visual Goal Mapping™ without doing the whole practice. Your brain will remember and do the work for you.

Stickies & Mapping:
Great Ways to Break It Down

This section has a lot of juicy information and exercises to experiment with. Approach each with curiosity and wonder, like a child with a new toy, versus a beastly dragon that needs slaying.

If this all seems like too much. No worries! That's why I've provided Goal Mapping: Great Ways to Break It Down. Here you will find a variety of random, simple activities you can choose from to begin the process of Goal Getting. Don't like one? Don't do it. If you feel completely comfortable with your goal setting abilities now, feel free to focus your energy on the honing your skills and skip the Great Ways.

Choose one per week. Practice several times per day, if possible. Remember my rule...Keep it manageable. Reward yourself often.

1. Practice doing the Thought Clearing exercise with new goals and projects, big and small.

2. Practice breaking it down. Take a regular project, like painting a room, and see how many steps you can think of to take it from idea to completion.

3. Practice estimating. How long do you think a task will take to complete? Note how close you came.

4. Practice timing current activities. How long does it take you to call a client, fold the laundry, make a sandwich, drive to the store? Becoming very aware of actual time is one of the best ways to put an end to over-scheduling and overwhelm.

5. Practice immediately scheduling tasks. For example, you realize you really need to pay bills by the end of the week. Instead of hoping to find time to fit it in, upon realization, pull out your calendar and schedule a time to do it.

Reflections on Stickies and Mapping

For some, this exercise can be challenging or overwhelming. It can bring up the fear of failure, not "getting it right," or missing some crucial, seemingly hidden step. You may get hung up on the "how"and struggle to move forward.

There are no tricks, hidden steps or competency tests here. You can't fail at this. You can only try, play and learn.

Rise above the storm and you will find the sunshine.
Mario Fernandez

Regardless of what this exercise means to you, but especially if you had any emotional responses, like frustration, anger, fear or overwhelm, please pause for a final moment to be with whatever emerged.

You might have experienced a panicky feeling in your stomach, clenching of your jaw, racing heart, or constriction in your throat. Conversely, you may have experienced joy, excitement or peace. Whatever it was, please pause and jot down your experience.

I have provided a few prompting questions to get you started. But again, I encourage you to observe any final thoughts, or enlightenment you experienced and capture them here. The thoughts you write down now will serve as a valuable point of reference. They may help you remember steps, insights or processes you need to keep in mind for the future. They may also remind you, when you are feeling frustrated with your progress, of things you already do well, things you need to let go of and more.

Also, later, when you come back and re-read what you have written, these thoughts can be a great source of proven growth. You may think, "Wow! I remember when I couldn't figure out how to…Now, my schedule is a piece of cake." It will become one more place to celebrate your stellar, amazingly fantastic self!

So, without going all "Dora the Explorer," and holding everything up to a magnifying glass, allow your observations to flow from your body and mind onto the paper: no filter, no judgement, no worries.

What did you learn about the way you think about goal setting?

_____

_____

What part of this exercise is worth doing again?

_____

_____

What emotions did you experience while working through this exercise?

_____

_____

What old stories, if any, came up while thinking about your goals, expectations, fears, etc.

_____

_____

Write one positive comment about yourself and your ability to set and keep goals. As with lesson in this book, something small is fine. For example you might be good at:

- Always brushing your teeth
- Keeping groceries in the house
- Meeting friends for coffee

What is your one positive comment. If you get stuck you can try:
I am good at...

_____

_____

Changing your mindset through affirmations:

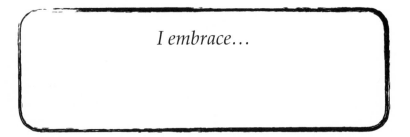

I embrace...

Need a suggestion?

Setting goals is easy for me. I make the time to be thoughtful and create a clear plan.

Random Thoughts About Goals, Stickies & Stuff

Section 2

Prioritizing

Create Goals

Make a Plan

Take Action

My Prioritizing False Start

When I began writing this section. I thought I knew exactly what I was going to say, the tools I wanted to include, and the stories I wanted to share.

With confidence and clarity, I wrote the whole first draft of this section, charts, exercises, and stories. I researched, selected and plugged in two well recognized prioritizing systems. Both of these systems were industry standards for decades. I was confident in their reliability and usefulness. In fact, I frequently use them when working with my clients. I added some instructions and stories as necessary, as I had done with the rest of the book, feeling certain this formula would work.

Fast forward a week or so, my husband and I began the deep editing process of the book, an endeavor we both found exciting and fun. We loved playing with word choices, challenging and testing concepts and transitions, talking through exercises and stories, until we reached that place of "That's it!" The process was simple, easy and remarkably glitch free. It was as though we were masterfully dancing the waltz, so perfectly were we in step with each other, my message and the project.

Then, we began editing this section on prioritizing, and suddenly our energy, conversations and thoughts became sloggy (foggy + sluggish). The dance was over. For the first time, I had feelings of frustration and a niggling fear that I wasn't up to the job of explaining this concept. In an effort to break it down, the descriptions were getting way too complicated and lacked the smooth transitions of the previous sections. I admit, I was disheartened, my dissatisfaction wormed its way into our editing sessions...and I wasn't the only one.

Where my husband had previously been very focused and engaged, now he needed to stretch his legs a lot, get cups of tea, and take short breaks to think. Something just wasn't working.

On day three, 20 minutes into our editing session, with a shake of my head, I put the computer to one side, looked at him and said, "This section just doesn't work! That's the problem."

"These are the wrong tools. They are too challenging for someone already struggling with prioritizing."

"It needs to be simplified. I need to start smaller."

Make a Plan

"That's it!" I said. "This whole section needs a rewrite." BAM!

A "That's it!" moment is one of clarity and confidence when you recognize that you can boldly move forward with the project at hand, knowing, without a doubt how to proceed. Suddenly, everything makes sense. The new path is exponentially easier than what you have been doing.

Take Action

And, with this clarity comes new found energy, confidence, and a renewed dedication to the goal.

"That's it!"

It's worth pushing the pause button on our discussion about prioritizing for this concept. Because "That's it!" is big...as in life altering big.

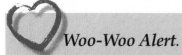

Woo-Woo Alert.
We are going to be talking about getting in touch with your emotions and listening to your heart. If this is new for you, just give it a try. You might learn something important about

When you get stuck or start feeling sloggy, it's time to push pause and ask the question, "What is called for here?", meaning, what *really* needs to happen now. You are not asking yourself what you *want* to do, or how you *think* something should be, or even what others are advising you to do. You are seeking the solution that is the perfect choice, in the perfect increment, that will guarantee success.

Another Woo-Woo Alert! What I know from working with my clients is that, more than likely, the answer is already within you. You just are not seeing it, hearing it, or liking it. This answer is rarely a "should do," as that's not your inner voice. For the most part, "should do's" are someone else's thoughts, rules or expectations.

Your inner voice is the voice of deep knowing. *That* answer is the best action for you. That inner voice, when really listened to, almost always requires less effort and leads you in the right direction.

As it pertains to this section on prioritizing, I didn't want to rewrite it. I wanted it to work. I had put in the time. I'd researched, planned, and written. But, the reality was… it just didn't work. It needed to be rewritten. Once I realized the truth, the way forward made perfect sense.

Here's the best illustration of "That's it!" I've ever experienced.

Recently, I was teaching a Visual Goal Mapping™ workshop. One of the participants was an older man, who slouched in his seat. He seemed somewhat deflated by the exercise. I asked if he was having a problem with his stickies. He said his goal was to be healthier and it had been for quite some time, but he had no noticeable improvements. Although he'd had 20 minutes to write all his thoughts down about getting healthier, he only had three stickies. They were: 1) Lose weight 2) Exercise and 3) Quit smoking.

He went on to say, "I knew all this already. I just don't know where to begin."

Now, I'd love to take three pages to diagnose this whole scenario, stickies and all. Instead, I'm going to focus on the "That's it" that took place because, it was priceless.

I began by asking if it was OK for us to focus in on just one stickie, the one that read "Lose Weight". From there, I proceeded to offer some suggestions as to how he could begin breaking it down to manageable tasks. My options began with a big change, which is how most people seem to begin, with subsequent options being smaller and smaller still. My options were:

1. He could choose to eat all his meals at home, making healthy choices, versus eating out all of the time. He listened, but there was no reaction.

2. Next, I suggested, he could choose to prepare just one healthy meal, like dinner, per day at home versus going out to a restaurant. Still no reaction.

3. Finally, I offered, "What if you choose to eat a healthy breakfast at home every Monday morning?" Immediately, his face lit up, he sat up taller in his chair and all but shouted, "That's it! I can do that!"

…That wonderful moment of awareness when the step you need to take toward your goal is so easy and manageable that you know you can't fail. It's the sweetest moment ever!

The point of all this is, when you find yourself stuck, overwhelmed or avoiding a task, it's probably best to pause and listen to see if your inner wisdom offers any insight on the cause of your struggle.

You may not like what you hear, like "this section needs to be rewritten." But, it is a truth. It is very real. And, it almost *always* makes the way forward easier.

If you are still confused, let me give you a slightly more in depth example.

When I was attending my first yoga training, three years ago, I experienced an amazing "That's it" moment.

As I mentioned earlier, due to life experiences my health had been rather seriously compromised. Up to that point I had been extremely active: rock climbing, road cycling, and snowboarding.

> **That wonderful moment of awareness when the step you need to take is so easy and manageable that you know you can't fail.**

That existence was no longer my reality. Although I prepared the best I was able, I could not participate in the training in my usual "all in", no holds barred, deeply physical way.

Even though I had spent two months walking, I was still weak. I had no stamina. I felt like such a failure. I spent huge chunks of our training in a laying down, restorative pose. I was deeply embarrassed and humiliated. And, I cried…a lot.

I kept thinking, "I'm an athlete, for heavens sake. But, I can't very well call myself an athlete if I'm unable to do 90 minutes of basic yoga?"

"Just keep going, you wimp. Power through," my thought monster admonished.

"Don't show them you can't do this. They'll think you are weak."

"Oh my gosh! What if I'm *weak*?" Good grief, what an awful word. What an awful reality.

For two full, 10 hour days, this inner struggle went on: attempting to participate, being too quickly reminded of my physical limitations, having to give in, followed by thoughts of failure, weakness and shame.

Then, day three arrived and I decided I'd suffered enough. I realized I had a choice. I could spend the remaining days bemoaning the loss of strength and stamina, the need to prove I was an athlete, *and*, subsequently miss out on an amazing experience.

> **Every time you say No, you make room for a Yes that really matters.**
> John Maxwell

Or, I could let go of my expectations and my old identity (as in who I used to be, and what I used to be able to do). I could fully engage in the training as I showed up, each moment, the new me, warts and all. I could, in fact, have the experience of a lifetime.

With that realization I thought, "That's it! That's the answer. I can make this easier. Or, I can continue to struggle. The choice is mine."

The remaining seven days things were very different. I chose to let go of old expectations and the inner struggle was gone.

When I took the time to ask, with an open heart, "What is needed in this moment?" the answer was right there. I needed to be real, as in Realistic, and let go of who I thought I should be.

It wasn't the answer I wanted. But, when I got to the point where I was willing and ready to listen to
whatever answer presented itself, everything changed for the better. My heart said, "Let go of the need to define yourself as an athlete and all will be well, easier, more enjoyable. You will have the experience of a lifetime." And, I did.

There were still tears of sadness. I mourned the loss of the egoic label "athlete," which had always been an integral part of my identity. But, the struggle was gone. The negative messages were gone. No longer was I a weakling or ashamed of myself for neglecting my health for the last 40 years.

Now, I was just Lisa, laying on a mat in Wyoming, trying to get her "OM" on, and rocking it! It was a place of grace, acceptance and peace.

The freedom a "That's it!" moment provides comes from a willingness to ask, "What's called for now?" then pausing to really listen.

"That's it! I can do that!" is a magical moment where everything makes sense. It's when the expectation is Realistic, the way forward seems easy, and the simplicity of the solution washes over you like a warm, relaxing shower. When that happens, there's a feeling in the deepest part of your being where...

You know

you have

THE answer.

As I write this I'm struck, yet again, that all the lessons I have been laying out in this book are always true... for everyone. Even me!

I started with a list of what should go in this section. But, the list was NOT enough. It was too vague. I needed to think more clearly about the tools I was using: who my audience was; what I was trying to accomplish; what my health and time would allow.

Prioritizing, was an afterthought. It was never the focus of my book. Goal Setting was. Time Blocking was. Prioritizing wasn't. Not that it wasn't important. It just had yet to fully appeared on my radar, yet.

My original plan for the book was to share my Visual Goal Mapping™, Time Blocking, and SMART goals. All of the other juicy tidbits were added on as I wrote, because they made sense and added better value to you, my reader.

Let's look at where I got gummed up as it relates to laying out the prioritizing section.

First, I wasn't Specific enough when laying out the details. I began with a section label that was too general. I chose Time Blocking without considering the need for other tools and preparatory steps that make Time Blocking possible, like prioritizing.

Consequently, I ended up with a section that lacked simplicity, one of the core values in my work. It also lacked focus, as the topic of prioritization was somewhat of an afterthought.

In planning, I hadn't been Specific about the content of the Time Blocking section.

Next, I wasn't Realistic. When I began to write this section, I thought, "I can find some tools from the net, and my library, add some descriptions, put in some real life stories. Easy peasy."

> **Every minute you spend in planning saves you as many as 10 minutes in execution.**
> John Maxwell

I realize now that this lackadaisical attitude was tremendously unfair to my readers. Who wants to or is going to read a book that hasn't been planned with thought and care? Certainly not me! And, I'm guessing not you either.

If I was including the topic of prioritization, I needed to be just as thoughtful about *why* it was important, keep it in alignment with my basic philosophies, be clear in how it was being integrated, and plan accordingly.

Unlike Visual Goal Mapping™, which I have written about extensively, I have never tried to write about prioritizing. I teach it. I talk about it. The process of explaining it in writing was completely new. Therefore, the complexity caught me off guard. I hadn't thought it through.

The end result…I experienced some minor and temporary mental chaos.

I felt overwhelmed, and at times, a bit frustrated. It is no surprise the initial thought of a re-write sapped my energy.

This initial set back also had the potential to make me very unhappy with myself. I could feel my thoughts wanting to go to a rather negative place. I started to hear, "You're really scattered!" "You never get anything right!" "You don't have what it takes to write a book!" Fortunately, I didn't buy into "The Talk."

There's a twofold message here. First, take the time to plan out all the steps; don't take shortcuts. You will save time and circumvent possible self-sabotage. There's an old adage, "if you can't find the time to do it right, when are you going to find the time to fix it?" Take the time and plan accordingly.

Second, if you do get stuck, and that can happen in the best of circumstances, be open to hearing a totally different solution to the problem. Be open to whatever comes up when you ask, "What's really needed here?"

The best practice in this instance is to continue to ask that question, reflect on the answers that present themselves, and reflect on those until you arrive at that magic place where everything falls into place, the way forward is clear and you can say, with confidence and clarity, "That's It!"

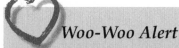 *Woo-Woo Alert*
Remember, you may not like the answer that comes up, or want to hear it. But, the answer is always there. It's always true. And, you probably need to listen.

Prioritizing 101

I attended a workshop, by a wonderfully talented Keller-Williams Master Trainer, on a concept called time blocking. In the opening, she zeroed in on a pet peeve of hers, the idea of time "management."

Her premise is that time cannot be managed. Time is constantly moving forward, chugging along at its own pace, refusing to be slowed or hurried. The skill we need to learn is how to manage our schedule and calendar, arranging our goals to fit in certain blocks of time, through prioritization, focus and intention. This idea is definitely worth further consideration.

There's also a somewhat new concept called Energy Management that's been making it's way into the news lately which is also worth some discussion. Energy Management asks us to consider how you want to use the limited energy you have. For example, when you are inclined to squeeze in one more phone call or meeting at the end of an already long day, you pause and ask, "Do I want to have energy for later? Do I want to calmly enjoy my family, my partner, or my free time? If I take this last task on, am I sacrificing my remaining energy store?"

When you choose to use your energy wisely, putting it toward those activities that have the most meaning and value in your life, you will find you have a whole new perspective on time.

Regardless of whether you find value in either or both of these concepts, you must admit it is an interesting perspective and worth further consideration. To create a more manageable schedule and life, prioritizing is essential for taming a chaotic calendar. The foundation of prioritizing is effective calendar, schedule and energy management.

> **More on Energy Management:**
> Invest your energy and focus on activities and relationships that bring the greatest reward to your life. Choose to do more of those.
>
> Eradicate activities and relationships that are a constant energy drain, or add little or no benefit. They are wasting your most valuable resource, the energy to invest in the rewards of life.

When I think of prioritizing and taming the chaos, I think of Donna, a new entrepreneur, opening a small, boutique-ish retail store. Due to the enormity of this undertaking, she began each day with pages of To-Do lists. In her mind, each task was equally urgent and important. She had several different ways of approaching her lists, top down, random selection, or based on time available in the moment.

Sadly, no matter how many tasks were ticked off, at the end of the day, Donna rarely felt as though she was accomplishing anything. She constantly felt frustrated, confused, overwhelmed, exhausted and defeated. The list never seemed to get any shorter.

"I've worked all day every day for weeks," she'd say. "How is it that I don't seem to get anything done, and I never get any closer to completing my big goals?"

In fact, she was getting lots of *things* done. The problem was the tasks she was working on were rarely those that moved her toward her Game Changer goals.

This is just one more example of a list not being enough. Donna had extensive lists. But, everything was of equal value. For Donna, responding to a random email request to upgrade her Amazon account received the same value as sending a quote for business to a valued customer.

That's where prioritization comes in. When you consistently focus on the tasks related to your Game Changer goals, everything...work, relationships, life, become better, because you are constantly moving forward on the things that matter most.

An important and final note on lists as they relate to prioritizing. A list is just ideas, notes, and things to remember. Your list doesn't become a useful tool until you apply some kind of prioritization tool or technique to it. In fact, if you are good at prioritizing, your actual "To do" list will contain no more than two to three tasks to be completed on any give day.

When you choose to use your energy wisely, putting it toward those activities that have the most meaning and value in your life, you will find that you have a whole new perspective on time.

**Enough, all ready!
Let's get on with it.**

Prioritizing Tool 1
The Highlight of the Day Practice

The simplest way to begin the practice of prioritizing is by employing what former Google executive John Zeratsky refers to in his book *Make Time*, as the Highlight of the Day practice. It's simple to explain and equally as easy to use.

Here's how it works. Every morning, before you jump into your work day, Mom day, whatever your regular day is, you take a moment to select the one important thing you want to Highlight for the Day. It could be absolutely anything.

Your Game Changers can be just about anything provided it brings the greatest reward to your work, relationships or life.

For example, you might decide that this day, you are going to Highlight finding the positive in people. Every person you meet, talk to, stand next to, or interact with in any way, you will find something positive.

I can hear your brain from here wondering how this could possibly have a positive impact on your productivity, Game Changer goals, or schedule. The answer is simple. You are training your brain to focus on one thing. It's really a mindfulness exercise. The more you practice the better you get at focusing.

Let's suppose your Game Changer goal is getting a new job. First, you might brainstorm the tools you are going to use to look for a job, for example, LinkedIn, job fairs, Monster.com. Once you have that list of tools, each morning, before you launch into your normal routine, you take a moment to choose one tool you are going to Highlight that day; and, (keeping your iSMART goals in mind) consider how much time you are going to spend at that task. Your Highlight might look like this:

Highlight of the Day: Job Search on LinkedIN
Time Alloted: 30 minutes
When: 2:30

That's it! That's the whole practice. Easy right?

 There is, however, a huge second, and potentially hidden reward. When you Highlight just one thing, at the end of each day you get to look at your To-Do list and joyfully check that box "Done!" You had one thing to do today, to spend 30 minutes on LinkedIn looking for a new job. Because you planned it, scheduled it, and focused on it, you got it done. There is no easier and more rewarding way to teach yourself to prioritize than by using the Highlight Practice.

I have a client that employs a very similar method. She has 2 rules. First, she can have up to three tasks a day. Rule two, she must be able to complete each task in less than 30 minutes. Once her tasks for the day have been selected, she writes them on a 3 X 5 card and tapes it to her computer or her refrigerator. As the day progresses, she takes great joy in checking off the tasks as they are completed and celebrating each check mark with great ceremony. That's absolutely delicious, isn't it?

Here's a sample card for you to use:

My Highlight Task for Today is:

_____

☐ I'm going to do this task for _____min./hrs

☐ I'm going to do this task at _____o'clock

I highly recommend the Highlight Practice for anyone who is totally flummoxed by the expectations of the day, and/or those who tend to over-schedule. It's remarkably easy. And, it can be amazingly impactful provided you keep the task in mind, keep the blocked time very manageable AND remember to celebrate.

Prioritizing Tool 2
The V.I.P. System™

If the Highlight Practice seems too simple, or you've already been doing that and are looking to take your list making to a more productive level, you may find this next system provides the extra oomph you have been looking for.

I crafted this system with simplicity in mind and with a strong desire to assist those who have no idea how to prioritize. It's a little more complex than the Daily Highlight technique, but of greater value, if you can manage it.

The V.I.P System ™ offers a slightly broader focus, allowing for more than one Game Changer task on your Daily To-Do list. If you read through the whole V.I.P System™ and feel overwhelmed, please just go back to Daily Highlights, until that practice becomes second nature.

Like all new habits, if you practice using this tool for a couple of weeks, suddenly your brain will understand what it is you are trying to accomplish and prioritizing will become automatic.

The key here is to learn the difference between Game Changers, meaning the tasks that move you toward a desired goal, and "squeaky wheels", those tasks that are distractions, habits and interruptions.

Sue was a woman on a mission, out to change the world one client at a time. As a large studio owner, her dream was to create a welcoming work space filled with practitioners offering a wide variety of wellness options.

Like many other new entrepreneurs, Sue's job required her to wear a million hats: scheduler, marketer, practitioner, seller and even receptionist. Getting her studio up and running, meant the To-Do list was never ending.

Remember, until you have done some prioritizing magic to it, your list is almost always longer than time allows.

When we first started working together, Sue viewed all tasks with equal importance, beginning each day with a two page list of tasks that she felt had to be done.

After listening, discussing and assessing, Sue and I attacked the chaos of her life by employing the V.I.P. Prioritizing System.

Notice: This is a…

> **Like all new habits, if you practice ... suddenly your brain will understand what it is you are trying to accomplish and prioritizing will become automatic.**

It's important to note here, prioritizing is like a lot of things. You need to be taught the basics to know where to begin and how to proceed.

So, forget all those thoughts about how terrible you are at prioritizing. The truth is, you just haven't found a system that works for you. My sincere hope is that one of these tools is the answer you have been looking for!

How the V.I.P System™ Works

Both Donna and Sue had daily task lists that included three major pitfalls guaranteed to create feelings of overwhelm, frustration and defeat.

Pitfall number one, when all tasks are rated of equal importance, it is inevitable that something truly important will be overlooked or forgotten. This creates unnecessary emergencies.

Pitfall two, since their lists were remarkably long and overwhelming, it is a given that they would never get everything done. This tends to lead to feelings of failure, focusing on perceived shortcomings and criticizing oneself.

"Why can't I make a dent in the list. I'm so lazy."

YUCK! You deserve way better than that. You are an amazing, hard working modern woman! You just don't know how to prioritize. But, you can learn!

You Go Girl!

The third and final pitfall, there's no place to celebrate. As we saw with both of our hardworking entrepreneurs, their wishy-washy, bulky lists were impossible to complete, thereby leaving no opportunity to reward themselves, to celebrate a job well done. Always create opportunities for celebration.

Neither of these lovely, talented women had a moment to catch their breath and celebrate a major, or minor milestone they'd finally achieved. There was no time for an excited "Woo Hoo!!!" followed by a relaxing "Ahhhh" that comes from a job well done.

Celebration taps into the brain's reward system. Failing to take advantage of this biological benefit is to ignore one of the most powerful, secret weapons available to you. Celebration floods your body with endorphins that excite your senses in a very positive way, allowing you to take on more challenging tasks in the future.

If Donna and Sue's experience sounds like you, don't despair. I promise, with a little practice, you will quickly notice some space in your calendar and a feeling of joy and calm in all areas of your life. Trust me, a life of constant success and celebration is just a prioritized list away.

Enough of why prioritizing is wonderful. Let's get down to…
…The How

Just like everything that's been described in this book, I suggest that you try the V.I.P. System™ for two to three weeks and see if you experience an improved ability to focus on your Game Changer tasks. Of equal importance, observe if you experience more positive energy, as well as more rapid progress toward Game Changer goals.

V.I.P. stands for:
- Very important
- Important
- Possibly important

Very Important tasks:
These are tasks that move you closer to achieving your Game Changer goals, or absolutely have to be done today, like paying on overdue bill, or your daughter forgot to mention it's her turn to bring snack for soccer practice today. These are always put at the top of your list.

You may never have more than three Very Important tasks on your "To do" list on any given day. Realistically, you'll only have one or two.

Important tasks:
These tasks still move you toward a Game Changer goal, *but* they may be able to wait a few days, a week or even a month before they need to be done. Or, they are simply less important.

Possibly Important tasks
These may need to be done, but most likely they don't move you toward your Game Changer goal.

Caution! Don't be fooled or tricked. Possibly Important items may just be "Squeaky Wheel" tasks, things that seem important because a Disrupter or Distractor has asked for them. Disrupters and Distractors are those individuals who impose the urgency of their needs on you and your schedule.

Example:
You have carved out 30 minutes to answer some important emails. You go into your office, close the door, compose your thoughts and...

Knock, Knock, Knock... "Got a minute?" Sam, your colleague, asks?

Uh-oh, Distractor Alert! This scenario is a situation I could spend three pages discussing. But, I'll stick to the subject at hand, Disrupter and Distractors.

Sam is a major Distractor in your office. He has no idea how to prioritize his tasks. Consequently, Sam's days are frequently filled with emergencies, which he seems completely unable or unwilling to handle on his own. Sam is also a yacker. He lovers to stop by for a chat and "run something by you".

I think you get the idea. Sam is one of those people who does not understand boundaries. If you allow it, Sam will interrupt you all day   long. His energy and noise will always signal a minor emergency. When, in reality, Sam's demands need to be prioritized.

Most times, Disrupters and Distractors need clear boundaries, boundaries that once established you rarely violate. These boundaries come in the form of clear rules as to when it is, and is not OK to be disturbed.

Once you create your Do Not Disturb rules, you will need

to discuss them with all concerned. Frequently, the hardest part about creating boundaries where none exist, is not with the Disrupters but, in training yourself to stay focused and firm.

For example, when my boys were still at home and I needed 15 minutes of quiet time, the rule I jokingly had for them was, "if you're not bleeding, don't interrupt me."

Disrupters and Distractors can be, but are not limited to, things like the ding of a text, random emails, phone calls, social media alerts and Drama Queens, like Sam.

More on Energy Management:
Distractors and Disruptors, along with unproductive or unnecessary meetings, are major energy drains, just to name a few. These items need to be on your Energy Watch List. They bring little or no added value to your life and take energy away from the people and activities that do. Be wise. Conserve!

Let's get back to the V.I.P. System™ and see how it will work for you.

Putting the V.I.P. System™ into Action

Let's begin by rewriting your original goal, the one you clarified with Your Big Why and iSmart goal system:

_____

_____

To demonstrate, let's suppose your goal is:
To write a book.

Imagine it's tomorrow morning. You just got up, took your shower and are sitting at the kitchen table, sipping your coffee, thinking about the day to come. Panic starts to bubble up. There's so much to do and not nearly enough time. "Have to's" and "Should do's" start flooding your mind, each howling for attention like a hungry puppy. The first course of action is to get all of this noise out of your head. So...

1. Create a To-Do list. Just let it all hang out!

    Making sense of your schedule (and life) starts with a Thought Clearing list of everything you think you have to do, you want to do, or you should do. Take a moment to jot down everything you think has to be done regardless of the time frame. This exercise is simply to clear your head.

2. Push Pause. Now it's time to add a little order to your chaos, and make some sense of the out-of-this-world demands your thoughts are creating. If possible, take a breathe, and just look at your list. Allow yourself to feel the enormity of what your mind imagines you can accomplish. Silly mind!

Your job, at this moment, is to realize how unrealistic your list may be and give yourself permission to consider the possibility that you can't do it all. Just because you thought it, and wrote it down does not mean it requires immediate action, or any action, at all.

In my experience, this list tends to be a whole, gigantic, enormous jumble of dreams, wishes, expectations, and should do's. Hopefully, buried deep amongst all the other stuff, you'll find one or two items that will actually move you toward your chosen goals.

If there's nothing on your list that relates to your chosen, Game Changer goals, congratulations! You've just learned something about yourself. You need to do a better job keeping your Game Changer goal in mind. If you don't think it, you can't do it.

So, if there are no Game Changer items on your list, add a task that relates to that goal.

Celebrate your new accomplishment! With great clarity and purpose, you have just made an important step toward completing your Game Changer goal.

Let's go back to our example of writing a book and follow this process through.

Your Thought Clearing list may look something like this:

___Sign up for next Project Management course
___Lose 20 lbs. by Jan. 1
___Work on intro to my book for 30 minutes
___Campaign to be on local board
___Contact Sue for interview on her podcast
___Pay utility bill, due today
___Shop for Tom's birthday present
___Brainstorm a title
___Redecorate living room
___Visit Mom and Dad

Don't worry if your list has dozens more thoughts, tasks and "should do's." That's really normal and a useful way to get everything out of your head. The above is a simplified list just to show you how V.I.P. System™ works.

3. On to prioritizing. At this point you are going to want to remind yourself of your one (for now, please choose only one) Game Changer goal. Look at your list and decide which, if any, of these tasks are essential to your Game Changer goal or absolutely have to be done today, i.e. paying an overdue bill. These tasks will get a V, for Very Important, next to them.

Here's how it would look:

Game Changer goal: Write a book
Sample Thought Clearing list with Very Important tasks selected:

__ Sign up for next Project Management course

__ Lose 20 lbs. by Jan. 1
V Work on intro to my book for 30 min.
__Campaign to be on local board
__Contact Sue for interview on her podcast
V Pay utility bill, due today
__Shop for Tom's birthday present
__Brainstorm a title
__Redecorate living room
__Visit Mom and Dad

There are only two items that warrant a "V" on this To-Do list, work on intro to book for 30 minutes, and pay utility bill that is due today.

4. Next, go back to your list and place an "I", for Important, next to any tasks that impact your Game Changer goal but may be able to wait a day, or even a week to complete. You can also place an "I"next to tasks that do not have a pressing impact or time sensitivity.

For example, the task, brainstorm a title, might get an "I" verses a "V." Working on the intro to your book is essential to the goal (V), whereas a specific title doesn't hold up the writing process. Therefore, although a title will be essential to your book, it can wait a couple of days or even a week to be created.

Game Changer goal: Write a book
___Sign up for next Project Management course
__Lose 20 lbs. by January
V_Work on intro to my book for 30 min.
___Campaign to be on local board

145

___Contact Sue for interview on her podcast

V__Pay utility bill, due today

___Shop for Tom's birthday present

I__Brainstorm a title

___Redecorate living room

I__Visit Mom and Dad

Visit Mom and Dad needs some iSMART work. Upon further reflection of this task, you realize that what you really need to do is look at your schedule for a free three day weekend. The sooner you do that, the sooner you can secure that date with your folks and get it on the calendar. You give this an "I" to remind yourself that if you get time today you could look at your calendar. If not today, it may show up on your To-Do list for the next few days. Ultimately, if it is very important to you to visit your folks, it will get a "V", and you will finally set the 5 minutes aside to find a date.

5. Finally, go back through your list and place a P, for Possibly Important, next to items that may need to be done within the next week or two. You can also allocate a "P" to random tasks that relate to other, less important goals.

Game Changer goal: Write a book

P__Sign up for next Project Management course

___Lose 20 lbs. by Jan.

V__Work on intro to my book

___Get pregnant

___Campaign to be on local board

P__Contact Sue for interview on her podcast

V__Pay utility bill, due today

P Shop for Tom's birthday present
I Brainstorm a title
___Redecorate living room
I Visit Mom and Dad

Although not a Game Changer goal, getting certified as a Project Manager is a goal you would like to achieve by the end of the next year. This task also needs some iSMART work, to be broken down into smaller tasks.

Since you have 15 months to complete the certification, giving this a "P" reminds you to take the first small step, which probably is making a list of all the subsequent tasks required in this process. You make a note next to "Sign up for PM course" saying *break this down.*

To see this concept through, your list of tasks for this Project Management goal may look like this: (each task showing up as appropriate)

- Find out when class is being offered
- Register for class
- Study for 30 minutes
- Study for final exam

Back to your Thought Clearing list, and how to prioritize Sue's Podcast. You want to be one of her guests right after your book is published. This connection needs to be made, as long as you make the call to her by the end of this month, it will be okay.

In the next two weeks, connecting with Sue will move from a "P" to an "I" as the end of the month draws near. You may get lucky and find a five minute window to send that email. By the last week of the month, if you haven't called or emailed Sue, contacting her will get a "V," because now it has become Very Important to make that connection.

Finally, Tom's birthday. It's not until next week. You may have time this weekend to shop. But, you just want to make sure you don't forget, like you did last year.

However, since you are a prioritizing Super Star, and have taken the time to make this thought-provoking, clarifying list, you realize you may be able to save time and gas by buying his gift today when you are meeting a colleague for lunch at the mall.

Congratulations! You have officially prioritized your list, turning it from random, unrealistic words on a page that constantly remind you of all you have not completed, to a concise Power List of tasks that are keeping you on track and moving toward your main goal, writing a book. You absolutely shine!

Coaches Rules About Your List:

Rule #1: Your daily To-Do list may *rarely…very rarely* have more than three tasks on it.

Rule #2: Your daily To-Do list will almost always contain one task essential to your Game Changer goal, even if it's only a five minute task.

Rule #3: No task can require more than 90 minutes to complete, unless you have cleared an entire day to work on it.

Rule #4: You may only have one 90 minute task on any given day.

Rule #5: You may not "stack" tasks, without a minimum of a 15 minute break between, unless your tasks are location based, as in the example of buying Tom's birthday present at the mall while you are already at the mall meeting a colleague.

Stacking based on efficiency works, such as same location, same tools required for two or three tasks, or same people required for two different   projects. Stacking events doesn't work when there is unrealistic cramming of random tasks into an already full schedule.

There's one more suggestion I'd like to make here. As described in the previous Highlight Practice, once you have V.I.P'd the heck out of your Thought Clearing list, it may be a good idea to create that most useful tool, Your Daily V.I.P To-Do list. You could use a 3 X 5 card like the one described in the Highlight Practice. This sacred list contains only the V.I.P tasks for that day in order of importance.

Here's a template you can use:

V.I.P Task	Duration	Time of day	Done

Here's how you fill it in:
- Write in your V.I.P. tasks for the day.
- Include how long you are going to do this task. *Remember the 90 minute rule
- Schedule the time you will do that task.

V.I.P Task	Duration	Time of day	Done
Work on intro to book	30 min.	2:30 p.m.	

Frequently, my clients find this practice makes focusing easier and makes their day more rewarding. Because their daily To-Do list only contains two to three tasks, they almost always have them all checked off by the end of the day. What a wonderful feeling of success!

It's important to call attention to the fact that some of the items on your Thought Clearing list didn't get any attention. This is what prioritizing means.

Your head is constantly creating new thoughts, tasks and goals. That's what your brain does. Your job is to take all the stuff floating around in there and make sense of it, sort out the good ideas from the bad, and the necessary from the unnecessary. It doesn't mean that you get rid of them altogether. Some of those tasks deserve consideration!

You have two choices when it comes to these non-priority items. First, should you have a few unexpected spare minutes…

and your V.I.P, or Highlighted task(s)
are done for the day…

you could chose to spend some, limited time, on one of these non V.I.P. tasks. If however, you find that you continually put this task off, it's time to put it aside for the future…in the Parking Lot!

The Parking Lot

The Parking Lot is a folder where you put your tasks, ideas or goals that you are not ready to begin.

For example, when you are sorting through your Thought Clearing list and you find that you continually label something a "P," for Possibly Important, or in the case of the Highlight Practice, you never shine any light on it, there's a good chance this goal or task is not a priority right now.

Don't despair. Just be aware! If this task has been on your list for a month or more, use your iSMART goal process to help you decide if this task is too big, too vague, or too soon. If it falls into one of these categories it might very well end up in your Parking Lot.

Here's how the Parking Lot works.

Create a separate folder labeled Parking Lot, where all non-priority tasks and goals go to be temporarily stored. Creating this folder will serve two purposes. First, you no longer have to keep putting it on your Thought Clearing list.

Second, and more importantly, you no longer have to keep looking at it each morning wondering why you are not getting it done.

I have found that my list making clients have dozens of tasks on their lists that keep showing up but never get any attention. Consequently, for them, it is a constant reminder of failure. Instead of focusing on all that they have done, they can only see all that they have not.

The Parking Lot folder is a great place to put ideas and tasks without throwing them away. But, as with everything else, there are rules to preventing the Parking Lot folder from becoming another wildly useless list.

5 Simple Rules of the Parking Lot Folder

1. If a task, thought or goal shows up as a "P" for three weeks without any progress, change in status or renewed energy, it gets moved to the Parking Lot Folder.

2. As soon as you decide a task, thought or goal goes in the Parking Lot Folder date it with today's date. This will help with sorting in the future.

3. Items in the **Parking Lot Folder** get checked once a month to decide if any tasks are ready to be moved back onto your To-Do list for today or the next 30 days.

4. Items that have been in the Parking Lot Folder for three months get moved. They either go back on your priority list with renewed clarity and purpose using your iSMART goal process, they become a Great Idea (more on Great Ideas later), or they finally get pitched.

   No reason to be an idea hoarder. Not every idea is a keeper, even though it initially feels like it is. Through this system you will come to realize those of real value and those that are not worth the mental energy.

Hurray!!! You win a prize for your amazing sorting abilities, and intellectual prowess!

5. The Parking Lot Folder may never have more than 10 items in it. *WHAT!!!?*

I'm going to make the bold statement that the whole reason you are reading this book is to make your schedule more manageable, and to have a daily To-Do list that makes sense, where tasks are reasonable and achievable. That can't happen if you continue to think that every thought you have is a great idea, that each idea is going to make you a millionaire, cure cancer, or save your business.

Our brains are idea machines. Occasionally, one of your ideas is going to be a real humdinger! It will be your next great product or service, get you that big promotion, or allow you more time with your family. But, a great number of the tasks and ideas that are showing up on your Thought Clearing lists are real duds, time suckers and confidence crushers.

If you continue to make long useless lists, you will continue to feel overwhelmed, as though you never get anything done; and, you will constantly be reminded of all you have not accomplished. That's an ugly, vicious, life-sucking, self-destructive cycle. And, it can stop right here and now.

Idea Hoarding is a no-no. That's why you are never allowed more than 10 items in your folder.

By using the Parking Lot Folder and its rules, you will have a system of sorting tasks that are truly worth keeping from those that are not. Remember, if you are not making time to move an item in the Parking Lot Folder back onto your daily V.I.P. list or making it your daily Highlight, then it's not a priority. You know that because you have done the work. This is not an arbitrary decision. It's based on good, solid data.

More About the Parking Lot:

Goals or tasks that end up in the Parking Lot are just ideas. Putting ideas here is not a sign of laziness, procrastination or failure. It is a magical place where ideas can rest, and you can learn about your creativity, impulsivity, ability to prioritize and follow through. However, this is short term parking.

There is one final piece to complete this practice...

The Great Ideas Folder

If you are following the prioritizing steps laid out here, to this point you have:

- Done your Thought Clearing activity.
- Created your V.I.P. list or Highlight task for the day.
- Noticed items that have repeatedly shown up on your V.I.P. list as a "P"and moved them to the   Parking Lot Folder. (Remember to date them before putting them in the folder.)
- Revisited your Parking Lot Folder at the end of every month, *removing* items that are older than three months.
- Confirmed that there are no more than 10 items in the Parking Lot Folder.

Now, what about the items that have reached the three month expiration date in your Parking Lot Folder, that are still great ideas, but not yet a priority?

The last stop in your prioritizing journey is the Great Ideas Folder. This folder is where your highest quality, non-priority Great Ideas live. Once a task, thought or goal has been in the Parking Lot for three months, and still has not moved back onto your priority list, you have the option of moving it to the Great Ideas Folder. Similar rules apply to this folder as for the Parking Lot Folder

Four Simple Rules for the Great Ideas Folder:

1. As soon as you decide a task, thought or goal goes in the Great Ideas Folder, date it with today's date. This will help with sorting in the future.

2. Items in the Great Ideas Folder get checked once every three months to decide if any tasks are ready to be moved onto your To-Do list for today or, the next 30 days.

3. Items that have been in the Great Ideas Folder for six months get moved. They either go back onto your V.I.P. list, they are re-assessed using your iSMART goals process (keeping it is not arbitrary), or you give yourself permission to let them go.

4. The Great Ideas Folder may never have more than 25 items in it, for the same reason as the Parking Lot Folder. You are streamlining your goal setting so that your schedule is more manageable and you are more productive.

Piles of Great Ideas are the same as long useless, overwhelming lists. You just can't get to them all. If you don't keep this folder under control, you will continue to feel as though you are not getting anything accomplished, or you are not moving forward.

Remember, idea hoarding does not serve the new organized, calm you. You have cherished this idea for three to six months without it becoming a priority. If you are still not ready to pitch it, revisit the iSMART goal process. If you are still struggling, here are some additional questions that may help you decide if this should remain in the folder.

- Is it Realistic to expect that I will get to this within the foreseeable future, meaning two years?
- Where will it fit it in my current schedule?
- Is this a wish or a goal? Do I wish it was done, but don't want to take time to actually do it?

- If I make *time* for this goal can I still achieve my primary Game Changer goal?
- Is this going to add to my ability to *focus* on my Game Changer goal or distract from it?

 **Be very choosey.** This folder is for the best of the best of your Great Ideas. With each viewing and sorting, you are weeding out the ideas that you have come to realize you are never going to put into action. This folder will become your go-to when you are ready to grow your business, go back to work, get a promotion, or take that next big step. These ideas are truly the gems of your brilliance! Be really selective about what gets saved in here. Your future self deserves that simplicity and clarity.

The biggest benefit of both of the Parking Lot and Great Ideas Folders is that if, or when, your thoughts drifts back to one of these "I'll get to it later" goals, you can calmly remind yourself that it's in the Parking Lot or Great Ideas Folder, available for consideration anytime you choose to make it a priority. This reminder acts as brain training which will slowly allow your mind to let go of those constant, disruptive reminders.

By implementing the Parking Lot and Great Ideas Folder practice, you have just freed up brain space and energy to focus on today's top priorities to create your best you!

To better demonstrate the effectiveness of this practice, let's revisit Sue to see the impact it had on her business.

If you remember, Sue was a woman on a mission, out to change the world, one client at a time. As a large studio owner, her dream was to own a welcoming work space filled with wellness practitioners. Sue needed an easy method to begin prioritizing her daily To-Do list.

Sue had collected so many great ideas that she was already keeping a great idea spreadsheet in her computer. The problem was, after three years, this spreadsheet contained more than 800 items. It was a daunting, bulky, burdensome list that had her constantly feeling like she was missing great opportunities. In her mind, if she *was* making progress in her business, she would already have put a lot of these ideas into practice.

Based on the many hats she had to wear, we decided the V.I.P. System™ would best meet her needs. Through continued practice and re-evaluation, Sue came to realize that although each day can begin with a wish list of tasks that *could* be done, the reality was, that when she focused her energy on her "V" goals, she had the biggest impact on her bottom line. Moreover, she had fewer emergencies.

She also chipped away at her "I" tasks and was constantly monitoring her "P" tasks, moving them off her list altogether when warranted.

She also noticed that many of the other un-prioritized tasks on her To-Do list were just ideas or dreams. By consistently implementing the Parking Lot and Great Idea Folder rules, strictly limiting the number of saved ideas, she was eventually able to whittle her spreadsheet of 800 supposed great ideas down to 50 real gems (Sue customized her Great Idea Folder allotment).

Sue finally became acutely aware that all the energy and time she was using brainstorming and cataloging her thoughts and ideas was much better spent working on existing projects.

Now, Sue is able to keep her attention right where it needs to be, on proactive business building endeavors, instead of constantly putting out fires and stockpiling not-so-great ideas that were damaging her spirit and self-confidence. And, the best result of all? Sue finally slept through the night for the first time in months.

Now, her studio is full of practitioners. With energy management in mind, Sue has hired a receptionist/social media person to promote programs and offerings, allowing her more time to practice her calling...massage. Of course, she has the occasional fire to put out. But, that's life. The rest of the time, Sue's life is more calm, orderly and manageable. She feels like a success...as she should!

Way to go Sue! You took control of your great ideas, list making and your life!

If life constantly feels like too much, there's a good chance prioritizing, schedule management, or energy management is a problem for you. By making one of these prioritizing practices a part of your daily routine for one month, you will notice a dramatic change in how your schedule feels, how your life feels and, ultimately, how successful, calm and confident you feel.

We all want a life, both personal and professional, that feels well ordered and makes sense. We want to feel as though we are gliding through life, making good decisions, being in control without being controlling, feeling calm, cool and collected. In that light, your prioritizing objective is to whittle your To-Do list down to no more than three focused goals per day, setting aside a very specific time they are going to be completed. All the other 'stuff' will get done... or not.

Coaches Comment:

In Control vs. Controlling: A very simplified definition would be; in control is when you are focused on how *you* behave and respond, whereas controlling is when you try to organize and orchestrate how others behave and respond. For example, if you like things your way, or do everything you can to get someone to respond or behave the way you want, you may have a tendency to be controlling. In an article from *Psychology Today*, Sean Grover defines controlling this way, "Rather than foster cooperation, folks with controlling personalities demand compliance" If you want to know more you can read the complete article Do You Have a Controlling Personality, on the *Psychology Today website*.

In the end, you'll feel great because you will be absolutely confident that you are always putting your Game Changer goals at the top of your daily list, getting rid of the unproductive "should do's" that are bogging you down, and creating an absolutely precious treasure trove of Great Ideas for the future.

Disruptors, Distractors and Boundary Issues: Prioritizing and Time Blocking Destroyers

 Kathy, a home based realtor, spent hours every morning responding to emails, taking calls and texts as they came in, and following up on social media. She just couldn't figure out where to get the time she needed to attend to some of her bigger business development goals.

During our initial consultation she was interrupted three times by phone calls or texts. Excusing herself, she answered each one. Not wanting to be insensitive, I asked if she had some kind of emergency requiring such constant and immediate attention.

"Oh no," she laughed. "The first call was my husband asking what we were having for dinner. The second was a client needing my mailing address."

Following her response, I kindly and respectfully asked her to turn her phone off until our session was over.

This incident was the perfect opening to talk about weighing the impact of her complete open access policy on her ability to focus on important tasks. I asked her to describe how intrusive it was to take every phone call or text as it came in. I also asked the impact these disruptions were having on her ability to build her business.

As expected, she was really frustrated with her family and their constant calling. They assumed that because she worked from home that she was available all day. Kathy believed she did not have an option. She wanted something different, i.e. for everyone to leave her alone, but couldn't figure out how to make **them** change.

Lesson one for Kathy, change always begins with you. I think that warrants repeating.

Together we talked about the Distractors, the Disruptors and her priorities. We evaluated what was having both a positive and negative impact on her business and her ability to stay focused. We discussed her best time for taking calls, answering emails and texts based on her energy, focus levels and client/family needs. This exercise created the foundation for much needed boundaries for an effective and efficient work place.

To complete this picture, we created a foundational practice for Kathy to be as productive as possible. This included a clear understanding of her needs and desires, and how to politely and respectfully inform her family and clients when she was available, and was not available.

It took some real stick-to-it energy. Her Distractors and Disruptors didn't want their access to Kathy to be limited. They were used to open access. But, once they understood the rules about when she was and wasn't going to answer her phone, (and with continued encouragement from me), Kathy was able to hold firm to her new boundaries.

And, no surprise…it worked, big time! Kathy identified her biggest, most impactful Game Changer activities and her best time to work on them. She established clear boundaries with family and clients and firmly adhered to them. The result of all this clarity and focus? Kathy won Highest Sales for the Month!

That's what I'm talking about!

I can already hear many of you thinking "That wouldn't work for me. My work (family) is different. It (They) requires... "

I have worked with women from a very wide variety of professions, including financial planners, insurance brokers and health care practitioners. This system has worked for all of them. It has freed up valuable time and empowered them to have greater control of their schedule, their energy and their lives. It takes a little time to put in place. It takes practice. And, it takes fortitude. But, you can do it. And...

IT'S SOOO WORTH IT .

It may be a struggle, at first, for everyone concerned. After all, you have been completely accessible to everyone, they now expect it. They aren't going to want to change. If you want things to be different, the change has to begin with you.

Remember, **change** always begins with **you**

There's a quote that goes, "You can't get what you don't ask for." Politely asking people to wait, call back during your administrative time, refrain from repeatedly calling during work hours about personal or family issues is not mean or rude. It is respectful of your time, work hours, and schedule. It is respectful of you. It is also more respectful of them. Once you set your boundaries *and stick to them*, those same phone calls and texts will get your full attention. You won't be trying to multi-task (another dreaded, highly inefficient practice). It is truly a win-win for all concerned.

Coaches Comment:

This is another gentle reminder to **take it slow** .It is impossible to implement everything in this book at one time. There's too much information and too many new habits to learn. Choose **just one** new habit, one exercise, or break down one section and focus on that small habit for three weeks, or until it becomes natural and comfortable.

Troubleshooting Disrupters and Distractors

 I have a "Sam" in my office, who just doesn't get it. How do I prevent him from being a Distractor?

Surprisingly, most people who haven't created boundaries have at least one Sam in their lives. Frequently, it's more than one. Setting boundaries in one area of your life will end up benefitting other areas of your life. Spend some time with this exercise to get you started on a life with healthy boundaries.

Creating Boundaries Exercise
or Great Ways to Break *This* Down

- Spend some quiet time thinking about what uninterrupted time might look like for you. Are your sessions once a week, every day, twice a day?
- How long is a particular session going to last?
  *It's important to be reasonable with time; restrict your Do Not Disturb time to 15 - 90 minutes depending on the age of your Distractors and the pace of your business. In a busy office, 90 minutes, during a non-busy time, is perfectly reasonable. If you have Disruptor children under the age of 7, don't expect more than 15 minutes of free time without the help of another adult.

We will talk more about boundaries, blocking time, and Distractors and Disrupters in the Time Blocking section.

Regardless of your chosen career path, life is not meant to be a stream of emergencies requiring constant attention and solutions.

Over and over, I hear women say, "That might work for them. But, my job is different. My work just has a lot of unexpected things that always come up."

Prioritizing works for everyone. And, it will work for you…if you truth the system.

Having read through these two systems, take a moment to think, with a new awareness, about your current approach to prioritizing. What small changes can you make to *begin* to affect change. Open your mind to the realm of what if… What if your schedule could be different? Would you like that? What if people would leave you alone? Would that impact your life in a powerfully positive way? If yes, these systems and subsequent tools are for you.

That being said, I can't emphasize enough, this is definitely the place to start really small. For example, although you have written down three goals, choose only one goal (a most important Game Changer) to consistently schedule on your calendar for the next week or two, in small time increments, (15 minutes or less), and notice how quickly you are making major progress.

Try it! It works and it's A-W-E-S-O-M-E !!!

A Great opportunity to remind you to…

Make it your own

Prioritizing: Great Ways to Break It Down

Remember, Prioritizing: Great Ways to Break It Down is designed to provide a variety of random, simple activities you can choose from to begin the process of prioritizing. Choose one or more that suits you. Don't like one? Don't do it. Do you feel like you totally understand prioritizing now?   Then, feel free to focus your energy on the exercises in this section and skip the Great Ways.

1. Notice how much time you spend on Filler tasks, i.e. random disruptive emails, phone calls and texts. (No new action required. No judgement, please.)

2. Each morning, before you get out of bed, take a breath, noticing where you feel the breath in your body. Do you notice air passing in and out of your nostrils, your chest rising, your belly expanding? Just continue to follow your breath for at least thirty seconds. The longer you do this practice the better you will be able to calm yourself on demand. Practice observing your breath every morning for two to three weeks before engaging in either of the prioritizing practices.

3. What does this have to do with prioritizing? A lot! One of the reasons we make really long, ineffectual lists is because we allow our brain the freedom to do what it does best, problem solve and protect. There's science behind the point I'm making. But, for simplicity's sake, when we allow our brain this kind of freedom it encourages our panic response.

    When we take the time for a nice, deep breath, experiencing it as fully as possible, it signals to our brain that we are safe. With that realization, our rational, executive function brain is allowed to think and process clearly.

So, if frazzled, frenzied brain is something you are very familiar with, this is the perfect place for you to start your prioritizing practice. Teach your brain to recognize who's in charge and capitalize on that amazing intelligence you have at your disposal.

4. Are you an overachiever, drowning in "should do's?" To begin your new experience with prioritizing, please try the Highlight practice first, getting really comfortable with focusing on just one special, or Game Changer task for the day. Once this has become easy and so automatic you don't even have to think about it, then you can move on to the V.I.P. System™. Small successes lead to bigger successes and better results.

5. For one week before employing either the Highlight or V.I.P. System™, notice your Great Idea thoughts. You have three options. Pick **one**. Track on a notepad, your phone, or computer how often you engage in one of the following thought loops..

   - The *number of times* Great Ideas enter your mind. OR,
   - Using a one (easy to let go) - three (very compelling) scale, *rate the energy* your mind wants to devote to this Great Idea, meaning how compelling it is.
   - How frequently a *particular* Great Idea interrupts your thoughts, nagging for your attention like a spoiled toddler.

Regardless of the option you choose, once the idea is noted, acknowledge it by saying to yourself, "Oh, that's one of those Great Ideas, I'm really clever. However, right now I"m focusing on this Great Idea...", filling in with your actual Game Changer tasks for the day.

For example, a random Great Idea comes to mind. You pause and think, Oh, that's one of those Great Ideas. I'm really clever. However, right now I'm focusing on completing the opening section of my book."

What does this have to do with prioritizing? Just like the breathing exercise from above, you are training your brain to direct mental energy to the task of your choosing. You, not your brain, are in control here. This may seem goofy or ridiculous. Trust me, it is a very powerful tool.

6. For one week observe, without judgement, and note when you feel overwhelmed, or when you are having thoughts of disappointment or failure toward what you *haven't* accomplished. Choose to note either overwhelm or disappointment/failure, whichever is your most common response. Not both. Track each episode with a (/) mark in your phone, or on a pad.

   If you'd like to take it one step further, note who is involved and how much prior notification you had (this will help you recognize Disrupters and Distractors). Please, No judgement here. You are simply collecting data and learning more about yourself in an effort to be better prepared, which should result in a calmer, focused, more productive you.

7. Notice how much time you spend on Filler tasks, i.e. random disruptive emails, phone calls and texts, social media. (No new action required. No judgement, please.)

Reflections on Prioritizing

What concerns or fears come up during this section? What tools can you use to lessen or eliminate them?

_____

_____

_____

_____

What words, phrases or whole sentences did you hear in your mind while reading about Prioritizing?

_____

_____

_____

_____

Does the thought of prioritizing create anxiety or frustration for you? Would it be possible to let go of the idea as a whole, of all your preconceived notions about yourself, and begin this process with just one of the Great Ways to Break It Down activities? Which activity are you going to commit to?

_____

_____

_____

_____

_____

In what ways are you good at Prioritizing? This may include:

- Eating a healthy snack or meal (prioritizing your health)
- Going to work (prioritizing paying the mortgage over staying in bed and eating bonbons)
- Brushing your teeth (prioritizing oral hygiene over the pain and expense of a trip to the dentist)
- Being nice to a difficult colleague or boss (prioritizing a job over no job)

Everyone one of us is good at Prioritizing certain things. You *are* good at Prioritizing. Now…. you will be better!

Write one positive comment about your ability to Prioritize. If you get stuck you can try:

I always remember to… (please note: *anything* you remember to do, that you have chosen to make a priority)

_____

_____

_____

_____

_____

_____

Changing your mindset with an affirmation:

> *I joyfully make time to…*

Need a suggestion?

I am great at prioritizing. I joyfully spend time each day choosing what Game Changer activity I will commit to. Then, I get it done.

Random Thoughts About Prioritizing

_____

_____

_____

_____

_____

_____

_____

Section 3

Time Blocking

Random Thoughts About Time

Frequently, those who struggle with time based activities, like being on time, completing tasks and being prepared, create a dialog in their head cataloging shortcomings and failures. If this sounds familiar, please take a moment to jot down how you feel about time, any negative messages you have or any fears that have come up as you prepare to read this section.

Time Blocking

Meetings, texts, email, Facebook, spouse, friends, kids, snail-mail, childcare, groceries, cleaners, doctors, exercise, shopping, travel time, eating, sleeping, personal hygiene…

What does your daily To-Do List look like? Does it have even more tasks on it than this? More than likely it does. The demands on our time in this fast paced, have-to, must-do society we live in are extremely high. Whether you are stressed or not by your schedule is completely within your control provided you take time to understand:

- How you are using your time?
- Who you are "giving" your time to and why?
- Where your boundaries are with regards to your time, your work, your family, and the most precious of commodities, your self-care?

As mentioned before, you may be familiar with the term "time management" in reference to how people navigate any given day, project or task. Instead of time management how about focusing on schedule management? Determine the time of day when you are most productive. Plan your most important task for those hours. Doesn't that sound more empowering?

With a little thought and a few tools, you can make a choice about your availability and create a stress-free schedule. You can set boundaries for your "sacred" time. In the end, you will have very clear Power Hours, times of peak efficiency and productivity, with a focused plan for what will be accomplished during that time. No interruptions. No drama. No chaos.

BOOM!

The Magic of Time Blocking

Before we go any further, let's demystify and clarify this concept. Time blocking is:

- A system of identifying your most valuable tasks, what I refer to as Game Changers, activities that bring the greatest reward (sometimes money, sometimes time) to your work, relationships and life. Time Blocking assures that these Game Changers *consistently* get the undivided attention they deserve.
- Flexible. You can always choose to adjust how you use your time and where your focus is going to lie.
- An approach, maybe even an attitude, as to how you want to live your work and life.

Time Blocking is **not**:

- A rigid schedule with no room for whims or creative detours.
- Eight hour days where every moment is scheduled.
- A long list of tasks that need completing.

Like most systems, there is a slight learning curve to Time Blocking. You will need to set aside time for the next week or more to implement the starter exercise outlined in the next few pages. It's important to note that you are going to be both creating new, life-

179

changing habits and letting go of some old, disruptive, non-productive ones. Any time we attempt to change a habit it takes time. Be patient. You may even want to go back and revisit the Readiness Chart to assess whether the time is right for you to take this on right now.

Getting Started

To use Time Blocking effectively, you must first understand where you are right now, meaning how do you currently use your time. It does not mean your schedule as you imagine it to be, you suppose it should be, or would like it to be. It is your actual schedule. As with the other exercises, this is going to take time. First, you will track your current schedule. Then, you will practice (notice the word 'practice') implementation. Some tweaking may be needed. You may find it useful to carry a Time Blocking pocket notebook in which you will note any observations. There will be lots of observations to learn from and your notes will be very useful as a reference.

Please Be Patient.

Be kind. Allow yourself time to create a new habit.

Step 1 The Time Chart exercise
Record your day *as you go* or, in a pinch, check in every hour and retroactively fill in how you spent the last 60 minutes. Pay special attention activities that are not work related like:

- Social media: Facebook, YouTube, LinkedIN

- Text messages
- Phone calls
- Email
- Personal distractions: coffee breaks, bathroom trips, laundry.
- Travel time to and from wherever

Research shows it takes at least 21 days to create a new habit

It's important to track a minimum of four workdays and one weekend day to get an accurate depiction of habits, schedules and time wasters.

You are welcome to create your own spreadsheet, or use the one provided. It is essential that you carry something with you, a pad, or your phone, and collect the information.

Daily tracking essentials:
- Guess-timating is okay, in a pinch. However, every effort should be made to record actual time per activity.
- All information is good information. No one is going to see this but you. Be honest and avoid judgement. This is a learning tool that will improve productivity. It is not meant to reinforce negative thoughts with regard to historic labels like lazy, goof off, ditzy, procrastinator, or slow poke. (No Judgement Zone)
- Don't wait for a new week to begin. You can start right now.

Time Chart Worksheet

TIME	Monday	Tuesday	Wednesday	Thursday
6am				
7				
8				
9				
10				
11				
noon				
1				
2				
3				
4				
5				
6				
7				
8				
9				
10				
11				
12				

TIME	Friday	Saturday	Sunday	Monday
6am				
7				
8				
9				
10				
11				
noon				
1				
2				
3				
4				
5				
6				
7				
8				
9				
10				
11				
12				

Step 2 Putting it into action

Pick your top three Game Changers. These are high impact activities that can be related to business goals, like top income generating activities. Or, they can be personal goals, like making healthy lifestyle choices, or spending more time with loved ones. Your Game Changer can be just about anything provided it brings the greatest reward to your work, relations and life.

1. _____

_____

_____

2. _____

_____

_____

3. _____

_____

_____

Step 3 Putting It Into Action Exercise and Worksheet

Repeat these 4 steps for each of your Game Changers :

1. Ask: What is your best time of day to accomplish this task? Before 8:00 a.m.? At the end of day? Pick the time when you are most energized and feel the most positive, capable and focused. *If there is an industry standard for this task please note that here.

   For example, one of my clients knows that cold calls are a Game Changer for her industry. Research shows that the best time to reach her prospective clients is between 9:00-10:00 a.m. and

6:00-8:00 p.m. This may not be her most energized time, but it IS the time this Game Changer activity needs to happen. We will talk about how to use this information to your best advantage later.

2. Ask: How long is your attention span for this activity? This question is really, really important. There is no right or wrong.

Make it your own

However, avoid using someone else's standard until you know what is right for you.

3.Using the "T" from iSMART goals, decide how much Time per week you have to commit to completing this task. Again, avoid using someone else's numbers here.

For example, Sam Sellers, the top real estate agent in the company, says that to be successful you have to make 80 phone calls per day. Sam is a single, workaholic. Sam's numbers are not your numbers. Find what your numbers are. Start small and create success. You can always make the goal bigger. In the case of Sam versus you, I'd recommend starting with 15 - 20 calls, just to find your consistent baseline.

To create a manageable schedule and life, honesty is essential here.

4. Block it. Enter it in your calendar as though it is a life-saving treatment. Sounds simple. But, let's take a closer look.

Putting It Into Action Chart:
Use this chart to record your answers.

Task	Best Time	Attention Span	Time Req'd

Step 4 Blocking it

You are almost there! Step 4 of the Putting It Into Action exercise is blocking your calendar. Based on the guidelines you have created for yourself enter each task into your calendar. If an activity needs to happen three times per week or once a month you choose when based on the feedback you collected. You are now ready to block it in. Here's an example of what your Blocked calendar might look like based on gathered info:

My three business priorities:

1.   Cold calls:
   • Client best time: Industry research shows 8:00-10:00 a.m. *Note: Allowing an outside influencer to dictate when something happens should not the norm. This is only OK when the outside influence is grounded in fact, not preference.

   Fact: You son's team practice is at 4:00 p.m.

Fact: Research shows the best response to Cold Calls happens at this time.

Preference: Client "I want you to be there to answer my questions as I think of them."

- My best time: 8:30-9:30 a.m.
- My attention span 30 minutes
- Four days per week

2. Networking
   - My Best time: Lunch
   - Attention Span: two events per month. *You must take into account your budget and tolerance for socializing.

3. Billing
   - My best time: between 2:00-3:30 p.m.
   - Attention Span: 15 minutes
   - Two times/day, Two days a week

Here's what your calendar might look like:

	Mon.	Tues.	Wed.	Thurs.	Fri.
8					
9	Cold Calls	Cold Calls		Cold Calls	Cold Calls
10					
11					
12					
1			Network Event #1		
2	Billing			Billing	
3	Billing			Billing	

Is That It ?

Yep! That's all there is to Time Blocking, in theory. The practice involves one more vital component. Commitment, or follow through.

There are two secrets to Time Blocking success. The first is schedule it as though it was a doctor's appointment that was providing a life-saving cure. Meaning, you don't make excuses to miss it. Remember, this is a Game Changer…your life depends on it!

The If/Then Solution

The second key is, what I refer to as an "If /Then" Solution, which works like this:

If I am unable to do _____(Blocked task)
Then, I will _____ (replacement task).

An "If / Then" guarantees that life **never** gets in the way of forward progress, of achieving the goal. The replacement task is usually exponentially less difficult and usually less time consuming.

Example:
Time Blocked Commitment:
☐ Emails at 10:30 a.m.,
    M, T and W for 30 minutes.

Create your If / Then:

Email If / Then:

> **If** I am unable to send emails at 10:30 a.m. (for the predetermined 30 minutes) **Then**, I spend 10 minutes before I go home for the day sending as many as I can.

To assure success, block a specific time, meaning, 1:00 p.m vs. by the end of the day. Life happens. You get tired. Don't leave it to chance, especially if you are a procrastinator. Be proactive by using definitive language in your Then statement. For example, replace "before I go home for the day" with:

> **If** I am unable to send emails at 10:30 a.m. (for the predetermined 30 minutes) **Then**, I will **immediately check my calendar and schedule** 10 minutes at…and get as many done as possible.

The most important thing about the If/Then is that the substitute activity happens within 24 hours of the missed commitment. Some proponents of Time Blocking say if you miss a Blocked activity you must complete the *entire* commitment within 24 hours. If you feel a strong dedication to a particular task, your schedule allows, or you are under a time crunch, feel free to apply an "all in" attitude.

It's my experience that most of us have way too much on our plate, our expectations are exceedingly high and getting it all done can be not only a challenge but a breeding ground for feelings of overwhelm and failure.

Therefore, if you are new to all of this, your schedule is chaotic, or you travel life in the frazzled zone please feel free to use the easier option of accomplishing a smaller portion. You will still enjoy a continued commitment to your goal which equates to a feeling of accomplishment and success... the true inspiration for this book.

Just in case you still aren't clear. Here's what an actual If/Then looks like from start to finish. First, you must imagine that this task is a Game Changer for you.

Time Blocked Activity: Game Changer Emails
Blocked Time: Tues. & Thurs. 10:30 a.m. for 30 minutes.

Pre-Determined If/Then for this activity:

> **If** I am unavailable at 10:30 a.m. for 30 minutes **Then,** as soon as I realize this is not possible, I will immediately get out my calendar and schedule 10 minutes to get as many emails done as I can before I leave for the day.

Here's how it plays out. It's 9 o'clock Tuesday morning. Your car breaks down on the way home from an appointment. "Shoot!" you mumble. "There's no way you are going to get home on time to do Game Changer emails."

Disappointment and worry well up inside. You think, "How am I ever going to meet my sales quota if I can't stick to my schedule?"

Suddenly, you are filled with joy and relief! Unlike all those other missed goals of the past, this time you are prepared. You remember that you have an If/Then Solution guaranteeing that you continue moving forward toward your sales goal.

The most important thing about the If/Then is that the substitute activity happens within 24 hours of the missed commitment.

You immediately pull out today's calendar (because that's built into your solution) and schedule a 10 minute session before the end of the day. At 5:00 p.m., instead of dashing out the door you spend 10 minutes getting your emails done. You rock!

You are awarded Salesperson of the Year! You are extremely thankful for this chapter on Time Blocking and send me a portion of your bonus check. We both celebrate our success!

Foul! More on Disruptors and Distractors

This section began as a Troubleshooter question. However, I quickly realized that it is such a major obstacle for so many people that it needed much more attention than a quick Q & A answer could provide. The people in your life can create the greatest distractions to your Game Changer goals **if you let them.** It's important to note that if it's happening, you are letting them interrupt you. They are not going to stop interrupting because you wish they would. This behavior will stop when you create clear boundaries and stick to them, like a drill sergeant.

Take a few minutes to note the consistent Distractors and Disruptors in your life.

_____

_____

_____

_____

I'm lost. How does this work ?

Let's revisit Mary Ann, my client who relies on cold calling to build her business. As it happens, Mary Ann had an open access policy. She was always available to everyone and it DROVE HER NUTS! Making cold calls is a Game Changer activity for Mary Ann. Here is how we implemented Time Blocking strategies.

Game Changer Activity: Cold Calls
Power Hour Time: (her most energized, focused time for this activity) M, W, and F, 8:30-10:30 a.m.

- By classifying this as a Game Changer activity, Mary Ann Time Blocks it. Because this is a new habit, she reminds herself of three important thoughts:
- This is a money-making activity essential to supporting her family.
- She is a good person for making this choice. She is not being selfish or mean.
- She makes a mental note to be committed to the "Do Not Disturb" status this activity deserves, meaning no...**No** disruptions or distractions.
- She notified the Distractors in her life, family and staff, that she will not be answering phone calls or texts M, W and F between 8:30 a.m. and 10:30 a.m.
- She created a special auto email, text and phone message to clients that says:
  "To provide my customers the best possible service I will be unavailable today between 8:30 and 1030 a.m. I will return all messages by the end of the day. " She even created an "If /

Then" for emergencies "If you require action before 2:00 p.m. please mark urgent in the subject line and I will get back to you by noon." Perfection!

We'd all like to imagine that it magically worked the first day. Sadly, this was not the case with her family The reality was her family Distractors didn't believe her. Why should they? Mary Ann was always available. In their minds, this new rule was for everyone else. Most likely, she didn't mean them.

Mary Ann was tested. But, with time, practice and reassurance she succeeded. She turned her phone on Do Not Disturb during her Blocked times. Her family finally understood that she really wasn't accessible during that time and stopped calling for trivial things. In the case of her aging mother, Mary Ann established a daily check in call at 1:00 p.m. Bliss reigned. Important work happened... uninterrupted.

What about her clients? Surely, they were upset. She must have lost business.

Nope! Shortly after instituting this policy Mary Ann had a record-breaking month in sales. Her clients had no idea they were a constant distraction. How could they? All they know is I call Mary Ann; she picks up the phone. In fact, it is your job to provide the best service for all of your clients. It is your job to focus on what serves them best. You cannot provide excellent customer service if you are constantly distracted.

With Mary Ann it's easy to understand her need to Time Block that activity. Research determined the best time for cold calls. Chances are your Game Changers will never appear in research and can be scheduled at your discretion.

Use the personal data you've collected to figure out when to Time Block these Game Changers. Then, set your boundaries. When your Disruptors and Distractors come along, they will demand their needs take precedence over yours. It's time to stand strong and call "Foul on the play. 15 yard penalty for interference!" All joking aside. If you want this goal to happen it has to be a priority over everything. **Period**.

Let's try an Example:
Time Blocked Task: 45-minutes workout M, T, Th, F.
Your Best Time is 7:00-8:00 a.m.

Your kids are 10 and 12. You call a family meeting and explain the new schedule. They want you to fix breakfast for them before school like you always do. Penalty flag for interference. They are old enough to fix their own breakfast. Your Game Changer activity takes precedence. Call a huddle. Plan to bake muffins on Sunday afternoons together for the week ahead. They get that homemade treat they love. You get to do your breakfast workout. *SCORE!*

Same situation, this time your children are three and five. The call here is a compromise. Pre-plan breakfasts for those mornings. They eat and watch cartoons while you do an exercise routine at home. *TOUCH DOWN!*

Time Blocking is about deciding what activities you value most and putting them first, including self-care. If you craft a plan that allows you to live and work guilt free with your attention *undivided*, then you can give your best to your job, your relationships, and yourself. You won't resent your Disruptors and Distractors because they no longer intrude. They respect your time because you respect your time. The result?...maximized time with your family and/or staff because you planned well.

Troubleshooting Time Blocking

 I need to spend at least an hour a day on one of my tasks but after about 20 minutes I consistently find myself doing other things. How do I Time Block this?

Good news! You are not alone. You are also not lazy, ditzy, or disorganized. You ARE an observant, self-aware person who has come to recognize where your limits are and are now able to proactively decide how to work within those boundaries. Congratulation you smart thing!

You have two available options. My suggestion is to try each and see which works best for you.

Option One:
You know you have to do one hour of paper work per day. Your paper work attention span only allows for 20 minutes per session. You Time Block three 20 minute sessions throughout the day.

Options Two:
For one hour of paperwork create a Time Block for 75 minutes. Do paperwork for 20 minutes, take a *timed* five minute break, come back for the second 20 minute session, take a *timed* 5 minute break, complete your one hour of paperwork. It's up to you to decide how much break time you need between sessions and adjust accordingly. Once you have instituted this practice for a couple of weeks feel free to experiment with your session length by adding three to five minutes. With time and practice it is very likely you will be able to increase your session length for this activity.

I find I am using my If / Then Solution a lot. Is this OK? If not, what do I do?

Continued reliance on If/Then Solution is another great litmus test *to* show where you haven't quite mastered the art of scheduling tasks, and estimating time. There are usually two reasons why you may struggling with this commitment. Reason One: And, usually the most common, you are too busy. Your life and schedule are too full. With an over committed, over scheduled life there just isn't room for life's unexpected ups and downs; so, you consistently don't have time to complete the task in its original format.

This question reminds me of Karen, a wife, mom, IT person at a large local firm and an entrepreneur (translation, two jobs). For the first four sessions, Karen would show up with a laundry list of reasons she hadn't implemented her goals from the previous session." On Tuesday, my daughter broke her wrist. We had to do the whole emergency room thing, then follow up doctor appointments. That day was shot! Then, on Wednesday, I had a project due for my office job and a big proposal, and final billing to prepare for my business."

Karen has too much on her plate. Life is messy. Things are going to happen. When you have every minute accounted for, there is no space for messes. Sadly, (Reality Check) you have to get rid of some things in your calendar.

Reason Two: It's no longer important. I'm not sure this needs any more description. Sometimes you will thoughtfully identify a Game Changer activity. You will Block It. You will even work on it for awhile. Then, you find twice per week you are using your If/Then. Pretty soon, you are barely squeezing that in. Don't despair. Use your tools to re-evaluate what's going on. Go back to your Big Why and see if something big has changed. You may decide this Game Changer needs to go in the Parking Lot for a month or two. When you take the time to explore what's going on, you will find there's no space left for feelings of failure. Understanding goes a long way to self- compassion. Please be kind.

Time Blocking, like any new skill, may take time to really understand and implement. The biggest challenge for most people is training yourself to respect the boundaries you set and sticking to them in the face of all the Distractors in your life. Once you've gotten a few successes under your belt true understanding and appreciation will occur and your whole world will be calmer, clearer and more rewarding. It's easy-peasy, lemon squeezy from there. When new opportunities arise, you'll quickly find yourself automatically checking and weighing whether it will fit in your schedule or not, drain energy from more highly desired activities or not, or distract from or move you closer to your Game Changer goals.

You have become the Time Blocking Queen of Your World!!!

Time Blocking: Great Ways to Break It Down

Remember, the Great Ways exercises are provided in case you aren't ready to totally commit to the whole concept of Time Blocking, right now. Use one, or more. Skip some. It doesn't matter. The idea is to build skills and awareness that ultimately lead you to easily and regularly using Time Blocking to simplify, streamline and supercharge your schedule.

Practice / track any one of these for one week:
1. Observe your energy level for a certain time of day, for example 9 a.m.-noon. Note if you feel positive, energetic, focused, overwhelmed, sluggish or easily distracted. If you like charts you can use the one below, or make one of your own to record your behavioral observations. You choose the moods/energy. If you consistently avoid an activity take note of that, as well.

   Use either a 1 - 3 or 1 - 5 scale to make tracking easier. with 1 = low.

Time of day	Energy	Mood	Avoided

2. If you are a "Git 'er done" kind of person track more than one part of the day, or the whole day. Like everything, make this your own by choosing what you track. Remember, observe and track:

   - Energy levels before nine
   - Energy levels before noon
   - Energy levels after lunch.
   - Energy levels in the late afternoon
   - Notice activities you continually avoid. Note the time of day and the activity.

3. Overwhelmed by the idea of tracking? Practice simply carrying a Time Blocking pocket notebook. This may sound ridiculous at first. But, I had a client that really wanted to employ Time Blocking, she just couldn't remember to write anything down, never had pencil or paper handy, etc. Her first assignment for Time Blocking was simply to carry the notebook *everywhere* for two weeks. Once that habit was established, and she did get used to carrying it, tracking her habits became a snap and Time Blocking unlocked her over-scheduled life. Be kind and start small! The practice here is all about intention. *You intend* to employ Time Blocking when you are ready.

4. Notice Distractors and Disrupters. When you are taken away from a Game Changer activity notice who or what has caused the disruption. (No Judgement Zone...in this case, of the Distractor. In fact, make this practice even more memorable by thanking them. In your kindest, most genuine voice, you might say something like:

"Thank you for that interruption. I am trying to become more aware of how I use my time. This was very informative." (Remember, no snarkiness allowed). Not ready for that? Then, mentally thank them for creating an opportunity for new awareness.

5. Notice when you are happy. *BIG ONE!* Make a note of what you are doing, and who you are doing it with. The more detail the better.

Reflections on Time Blocking

What fears came up? What can you do to address these fears?

_____

_____

_____

What words, phrases or whole sentences did you hear in your mind while reading about Time and Time Blocking?

_____

_____

_____

Is the idea of Time Blocking causing you anxiety or frustration? Would it be possible to think of time differently for just one day, or one part of the day? Can you commit to just one of the Great Ways to Break It Down activities? If so, which activity are you ready to try?

_____

_____

In what ways are you good at observing and valuing time? This may include:

- Sending birthday cards on time
- Being an excellent baker or cook
- Dancing or singing with the beat
- Making people laugh (timing)
- Being there to support a friend

Write one positive comment about yourself and how you manage time. If you get stuck you can try:
I am learning to…

_____

_____

Changing your mindset with an affirmation:

> *It is easy for me to…*

Need a suggestion?
Time is my best friend. I am always prepared and show up on time.

Random Thoughts About Time & Time Blocking

Section 4

Work Life Integration

The Mindfulness Connection

Work Life Integration:
The Mindfulness Connection

I would feel negligent if I didn't at least mention the importance and impact mindfulness can have on productivity, goal accomplishment and a more manageable life. If you want to slow down your life, Mindfulness is the answer. It connects you to your thoughts, your purpose and your world. It's the pause you are looking for every moment of every day. It's easy to do and requires no special clothes, equipment or teacher. It's just you with yourself. That's it.

What Is Mindfulness?

There's a lot of talk about mindfulness these days. Like most things there's some truth and some absolute weirdness surrounding this topic. It's worth spending a moment to clarify what I mean by mindfulness and why it's important. Let's begin with a basic understanding:

Mindfulness Is:

- Paying attention to what is in the moment without judgement or direction
- Awareness
- A new-ish movement in the field of mental wellness
- An effective treatment or practice for pain, anxiety, depression and stress
- A way to identify thought patterns, both negative and positive, and to provide "space" for choice
- Living in the present

- Brain training that works to avoid habitual responses
- Scientifically proven to have positive effects

Mindfulness Isn't:

- Airy-Fairy Woo-Woo stuff
- A religion or cult
- An effort to *stop* "bad" thoughts or a busy mind
- A Forced clearing the mind
- Something you do in a weird posture wearing unusual clothes
- Weird breathing practices

Why is Mindfulness included in this book?

As I have worked on developing my business coaching practice, I have also been developing my own mindfulness practice. My journey began with Louise Hay's book *You Can Heal Your Life*, which exposed me to the wonderfully valuable world of self-worth and the power of affirmations. From there I moved onto Tal Ben-Shahar's book *Happier*, a beautifully written guide, where I learned to be happy with what *is* verses constantly driving toward the next big accomplishment.

Still hungry, I continued reading, enjoying my new found awareness and contentment. Little by little things began to change. Life slowed down. Relationships changed, my health started to improve and my business took root.

I continue to share my journey here because I want you to know I have walked this path and lived a stressful life to the point of making myself ill. Mindfulness opened the doors for big change. When self-doubt and judgement arose, and it did continued to rear its ugly head, I mindfully decided it wasn't useful and put it aside. I became open to the question, "Who am I right now, in this moment." And, I'd work from there. During the times when energy was very low or anxiety was very high, the question became, "What can I accomplish right now, in this moment?" Sometimes, the answer was "Absolutely nothing." And, I was able to accept that reality.

Mindfulness allowed me the space to hear the judgement, criticism, the old stories...

> ...and
>> my
>>> truth.

It provided the tools to see these as just thoughts and not my identity and not my tomorrow. Just my today.   Just my now. Mindfulness provided me the foundation to be me, just as I am. No labels necessary. Just me.

For me, and millions like me, mindfulness is the key that gives me the power to make order out of chaos, and allow space and reason to prevail when life becomes overwhelming. I know, because I live it, coach it, and see it happening over and over again.

That's why mindfulness
is a part of this book,
and may be a valuable tool in your life.

So how do I begin this mindfulness thing?

Do you have 5 seconds to close your eyes and take a breath? If the answer is "yes" then that's where you begin. Set aside just a few times a day to pause, turn off the phone, you may want to close your eyes, and simply take a breath, listening and feeling the inhale and exhale. Feel and listen. That's it!

If your answer was "no," and for some it will be, that's OK too. Because in recognizing that you don't have those 5 seconds, you have also begun the journey of mindfulness. You were in the moment long enough to consider this question and answer honestly. Congratulations! For you, the first step is just noticing if you are breathing. Can you feel the rise and fall of your breath? Yes? Welcome to mindfulness. It's that easy to begin, and it can grow to permeate as much of your life as you want it to.

My goal in introducing mindfulness here is that I find it is an essential element to goal success. When you are more calm, more focused and life makes more sense, goals happen.

What follows are some very easy ways to introduce mindfulness into your life. Take a moment right now, literally 30 seconds, or less, to play with the idea of mindfulness.

In This Moment Exercise

Mindfulness is all about being in the moment. In This Moment is so simple, anyone can do it! All you have to do is remember to stop, put everything down, away and off, and listen. In this moment:

- What do you hear?
- What do you see?
- What do you smell?
- What do you feel, inside and out?

The beauty is, it only takes a moment.

As with all mindfulness practices, remember that it is normal for your focus to wander. When you find yourself making a shopping list or worrying about the project due tomorrow think, "that's a thought. Right now I prefer to focus on…" (insert mindfulness activity of choice, like smelling) and gently guide your mind back. This is very definitely a No Judgement Zone.

Other Mindfulness Practices

Out and About

No matter where you are or what you are doing it's easy to have a mindful moment.

- This is what it feels like to...
  One of my favorites! Anytime, anywhere... stop and say, "this is what it feels like to..." and fill in the blank. This works best if you are very specific. You may need to look up a list of emotions to better describe what it is you actually are feeling. FYI, using words like "good" won't count. Be more specific.

- Actions speak louder that words
  Take a moment to be nice to a stranger. Hold a door. Be nice when they are not. Rake their leaves. Shovel their driveway. Smile. There are a million little (and not so little) ways that we can show we care. *Note: you can't do this one with the expectation that you are going to get anything in return. Like all mindfulness exercises you are doing it just for the experience. Having expectations ruins the magic.

In the office

Work can be very demanding, texts dinging, email coming in, invoices to be sent and paid. The call for action and attention is constant. What better place to insert a moment of calm.

- Observe how the pen feels in your hand as you are writing, the drag of the point on the paper. Which fingers are doing the work? Where do you feel the pressure of the pen?

- Pause. Close your eyes. Without seeking or searching, notice any noises that occur. No need to label them "door slamming" or "arg! Sam is always really loud." Just notice the quality of the sound. Is it deep? Prolonged? Staccato?

- Close your eyes. Take a normal breath. Then, notice: What do you smell? What sounds do you hear? Is there a taste in your mouth? What do you feel both inside and outside your body?

In the kitchen
The process of harvesting, buying, prepping and cooking food is a veritable smorgasbord of mindfulness opportunities.
- Chop, peal, slice
  Eyes wide open for this one! Focus on your knife, how smoothly does it glide? Or, not? The textures and shape of the food in your hand. There is a wide variety of wonderful experiences here. Notice all the different sensations.

- Food-tastic!
  Everyone loves food of one type or another. But, have you ever tuned the rest of the world out and really noticed all the different experiences available from eating. Observe temperatures, texture in your mouth, texture in your hand, appearance on your fork, smells, the number of different tastes. Step right up! The buffet is always open.

You have the idea. Mindfulness can happen anywhere, anytime. Once you start purposefully observing the little things in life with no judgement, criticism, or expectation, you will find that the choice is available in other areas when you are not even pausing. Your mind has been trained to be more observant and be openly curious. It will prompt you to ask, "What's really going on here? How do I genuinely feel?" New choices will arise. New behaviors will be possible. That's when you will know it's working.

Things I'd Like to Remember About Mindfulness

_____

_____

_____

_____

_____

_____

_____

_____

_____

_____

_____

_____

_____

_____

_____

_____

Raising Your Mindful Awareness

Create a list of prompts that inspire you to engage more deeply with yourself, your body and your daily routine. As you get the hang of this, refine your list to best reflect areas that need more thought and awareness. For example, if you get to the end of every day and realize that you never paused to celebrate, make this your priority for tomorrow. Here are some more ideas to get you started:

- When I close my eyes and reflect on the day, does anything significant stand out? Did something noteworthy happen?

- Does my mood or energy change at different times of the day? Was there something specific that affected my mood? If yes, what was it? Or, do I consistently experience ups and downs at the same times?

- Did I spend any time today *just for me*?

- Did my schedule feel more manageable? What did I do differently to make that possible?

- Did I have a preconceived idea about something or someone that kept me in a "box"?

- Did I pause when someone asked me to do something that I really didn't want to do (and truly didn't have to) and examine the source of the discomfort? Did I respond both honestly and mindfully? Possibly even saying, "No, I am unable to help." If you said yes, how did that feel? (No Judgement Zone)

- Was I overwhelmed by my thoughts?

- Was there a thought that was worrying me? Did I observe any sensations in my body associated with this worry?

- Did I pause to acknowledge a completed task, a job well done?
- Did I experience love? (Don't be tricked by this one. I'm not referring to grand gestures. It is a subtle awareness of the love that is all around us. I define love here as someone noticed me, even if it was just to open a door, a passing smile. Or, I noticed someone and smiled. It could kind words to yourself, or an act of self-care. This one is absolutely and completely about looking for the love that *is* in the world. If you look for it you will find it.)

Try to answer a couple of these questions, either through journaling or just quiet contemplation, before you go to bed to stay on track and keep your life in the calm lane.

When you bump up against a struggle or an old, unwanted habit, there's no need for judgement or criticism...or even frustration. Instead, congratulate yourself on your new found awareness and dedication to learning. Then, set a positive intention for the next day knowing every day is a new chance to begin again.

Troubleshooting Mindfulness

There are no Troubleshooting questions for this section because mindfulness is just a practice. You can't get it wrong. The whole point of mindfulness is just to experience the moment. Practice the exercises in this Section without expectation and just for the experience. By doing so, you are on your way to establishing a great practice.

If an issue or concern has come up for you please feel free to write it down here. You are welcome to email me with questions at LisaS@LisaStearns.com

Observations and Challenges

_____

_____

_____

_____

_____

_____

_____

_____

_____

_____

_____

_____

Mindfulness: Great Ways to break It Down

Remember, Great Ways activities offer a variety of options for you to tippy toe your way into a new skill. There is no order to these suggestions. Feel free to select the practice that is most inspiring.

All the practices in this section are designed to be easily incorporated into a busy day. That being said, here are even more mindfulness activities. Practice one of these for a week, or more, if possible several times a day.

1. Pause. Take two breathes feeling the in breath and the out breath.

2. Stop what you are doing and feel the texture of the surface you are sitting on. Describe the surface using as many words as possible.

3. Observe when anger arises. Pause. Describe where you are feeling the anger: In your stomach? Chest? Throat? Is breathing difficult? Just observe.

4. Observe when joy arises. Pause. Where are you experiencing this feeling. Sit with it noticing all of the sensations that arise. Try not to be in a hurry to move on to your next activity.

5. One of my fav's… when in public, listen for a child's laugh and savor it. See if you can feel their joy. Allow that innocent happiness to permeate your spirit.

Once you get the idea feel free to create you own Pause Moments. There are a thousand opportunities a day to stop and notice.

Reflections on Mindfulness

I smiled as I got ready to write this because the practice of mindfulness is an exercise in reflection and observation. Upon further thought and examination, I realized that if mindfulness is a big, new, unknown concept for you there may be a lot of thoughts and emotions that come up with this practice. Please consider simply pausing for reflection.

If you already enjoy a mindfulness practice, you may appreciate the opportunity to pause for reflection on this experience as well.

What was your initial thought upon first seeing mindfulness included in a business/productivity type book?

_____

_____

_____

_____

Did any thoughts or fears come up for you? Fear of failure? For example, did you hear yourself thinking "I could never quiet my mind." Or, "This is goofy!" Did you find you had expectations, your own, or that of others? Can you capture any of those thoughts?

_____

_____

_____

_____

_____

What internal, physical experiences did you observe while doing the In This Moment exercise?

_____

_____

_____

_____

Frequently, if you have been labeled flighty, ditzy, spacey or other similar words, you come to think that you are incapable of focusing. Not true! There are many everyday activities that require great focus, or we might cut ourselves, burn ourselves, or drive off the road.

What activities do you currently participate in where you have demonstrated great focus, meaning you are able to pay great attention to detail? It may be something as simple as:

- Shaving your legs
- Cooking
- Reading to your child
- Jewelry making
- Artistic endeavors
- Holding a little child

Write one positive comment about yourself and how you are already mindful.. If you get stuck you can try:
I really pay attention when I…

_____

_____

Changing your mindset with an affirmation:

> *I take time to...*

Need a suggestion?
I am calm and focused. I love being fully engaged in just one activity.

Random Thoughts About Mindfulness

Section 5

Celebration

Celebration: The Ultimate Act of Self-Love

Congratulations! It's time to celebrate! You made it through to the end! You've worked hard. Well done!

All good effort needs to end in celebration. In our fast paced world of high expectations, bigger, better, faster, stronger...pausing to appreciate what we have has completely gotten lost. If you are not careful life can become a crazy-fast hamster wheel of doing, where you are constantly running full steam ahead to the next project, the next activity, the next big thing, no longer sure where it is you are actually going.

Celebration is the ultimate act of love and self-care. It is the time you take to pause and acknowledge a job hard fought, a goal well met, a task well done. It is the place where new energy comes from, where self-confidence is built and you realize your magnificence.

When I talk about celebration with my clients I frequently hear two things. The first is, "I don't have money for that." And two, "I don't have any idea what to do." The fact of the matter is that all you need to celebrate is a pause, a moment that you stop, look for and notice positive feelings that arise from completion and cherish them. Give them time to run their course and blossom.

Celebration is the ultimate act of love and self-care.

There are a million little ways to celebrate that require little or no money. Here's a list you can choose from until the act of celebrating becomes a habit:

1. Sit quietly and breathe in the feelings bubbling inside while repeating, "Great job! You saw this all the way to the end. You rock!"

2. Call a friend and say, "I just needed to share. I'm celebrating the completion of…You are always there for me. I wanted you to be a part of this success."

3. Create a FB post, "I'm celebrating the completion of …" just to put it out there…to the Universe. No acknowledgement necessary.

4. Invite friends to join you for ice cream, a drink, a walk or pizza.

5. Take a bubble bath.

6. Give yourself permission to take some time off from obligations even if it's just 15 minutes.

7. Here's one of my favorites from one of my clients. She rewarded herself with a fancy bar of soap (a luxury she couldn't normally justify) and whenever she wanted to celebrate she would use her special soap. Squeaky clean and jubilantly celebrating success all at the same time!

8. Mani-pedi

9. Walk in nature

You get the point. Whatever brings you joy. Find a moment to appreciate your efforts. Allowing yourself a 'Well Done' when you've worked hard forces you to recognize that you have stayed on task, overcome obstacles and actively contributed, in a positive way, to your mission. All those things are amazing! That means you are amazing! When you recognize that you just might be just a little bit amazing, confidence grows. When you share your celebration you give others the permission to see their greatness. You become the light.

Coaches Comment:
You get to celebrate a good effort, a task completed. You are allowed to change your definition of success as you go. There is no judgement allowed at this party. Just good old fashion cheers all around for continually showing up.

Simple things I can do to celebrate:

_____

_____

Tasks and Goals I completed and forgot to celebrate.

_____

_____

Troubleshooting Celebrating

 I don't even know what you are talking about. I'm always just moving on to the next big thing. Do I really need to celebrate?

Absolutely! There are few people that need to learn to celebrate more that the chronic achiever. When you constantly chase the goal, you are actually chasing after a feeling. It might be a feeling of success, worthiness, value, or intelligence, whatever drives you. The question becomes, when is it enough? When are you enough?

There's a great book called *Happier*, by Tal Ben-Shahar, in which he describes this experience first hand and the damage it can cause to your state of happiness. He contends, and I agree, that happiness, success, "good enough," worthiness, whatever you are seeking, is built into each and every activity we engage in. When we learn to celebrate each moment we come to celebrate life!

So, go ahead. Push pause and pat yourself on the back for a job well done, no matter how big or small the task.

 How can I possibly celebrate the small stuff. I'd feel stupid!

First, re-read the previous troubleshooting question. OK, now let's add a little more juice to this topic. Celebration is a glorious activity, full of happiness and gratitude. Many people even have Celebration of Life when a loved one dies. There are no rules or limits on joy. Just like the big tools you have learned throughout this book, if this is a new concept for you then start very small. For example, you might begin with a random, "Hooray for me!" because you got out of bed, went to work, or fed the dog.

When a simple task is completed just say a small Hooray! And see how it feels. You can work your way up to bigger and better things as you become more comfortable.

I experienced one of my first whole body, joyful moments of success when I completed the first , unedited writing of this book. I have been practicing for years celebrating the little things, which did, on many a day include getting out of bed.

Completing this book was the first time I have ever said, "Oh my gosh, I'm done!" and I felt the tingle in my belly and heart space. It spread throughout my chest, thrilled it's way up my throat, producing a rather shy smile, resulting in a self-conscious giggle. Wow, I thought! This is what success feels like. This is what loving myself feels like.

My initial thought, upon completion was to rush into the next thing, editing, looking for images, creating a list of what needed to come next. Instead, I paused and took in the whole yummy, warm, tingly, giggly experience. And, it was delicious!

No one is too successful, too busy, or too important to celebrate. Pausing to say, "Well done!" is truly one of the best gifts you can give yourself; because, whenever you say, "Good job!" it is revitalizing and a confidence builder. You know without a doubt that you have traveled a journey and through the challenges, sadness, hardship, pain, and busyness, you actually made it. That's amazing!

Great Ways to Break It Down

There really is only one Great Way for this activity. Stop and notice when you have completed something...ANYTHING. Just stop and say, "Good Job!" and feel the joy radiating out of your heart space.

Reflections on Celebrating

Just like all the other tools in this book, celebrating is learned. If you currently do not have a celebration practice then start really small.

What thoughts came up for you about celebrating? Take time with this reflection. It's important.

_____

_____

_____

_____

Are there tasks and goals you completed in the last week, month, or year that you forgot to celebrate? What were they? Why didn't you take time to celebrate the completion of this project?

_____

_____

_____

_____

Is there one simple way you can celebrate one of those successes today? (Hint: it can be as simple as thinking about the project and what your contribution was, then giving yourself a mental "Atta girl" for a job well done..._even if it didn't come out the way you wanted!_)

_____

_____

_____

_____

Changing your mindset with an affirmation:

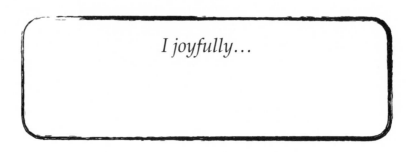

I joyfully…

Need a suggestion?
Because I love myself I remember to celebrate my successes, big and small.

More Random Thoughts About Celebrating

Section 6

You Did It!

We Have Reached Our Final Destination...

Much like a three day training, you may be experiencing that supercharged feeling you get when your mind is full of new ideas and the power of possibility. Go with it. Mindfully. There is a lot of information in these pages. If your habit is to gobble your way through life, consuming new ideas with gusto, I'm going to encourage you to pick just one section and work on it until it feels really natural. Then, you can come back and take on another. In this way, you will find the tools will be easier to implement and new habits will be established with less effort. The methodologies will become second nature, creating a great foundation for true and lasting change.

If, on the other hand, you are experiencing feelings of overwhelm, peppered with a wee bit of fear, and you're hearing phrases like, "Ahhh... where do I begin?" "What if it doesn't work?" "What if I'm stuck being disorganized and overwhelmed?", then it's time for a coaching comment. My suggestion is the same as it has been throughout our journey. Start with just one small new activity, like those found in one of the Great Ways pages. Or, just practice the stickie Thought Clearing exercise, getting everything out of your head. Practice makes perfect. You get the idea. Take a nibble, not a bite!

Serena Williams wasn't born the number one Women's Tennis champion. It took her hours and hours of practice to perfect her game. Practice can help ramp up your game as well.

Practice and observe. Be curious about your stickies, what they say, where you are putting them and how you order them. Become intimate with how you think about time, your availability, your necessity to say "yes" to every request. Practice mindfulness and huge opportunities for change will present themselves.

Realistic. As you think about all of these wonderful tools and how they are going to slow down your life and make it more manageable, keep your expectations realistic.

When I teach these tools to my clients we work on them for *months*, together. That means I am there to troubleshoot glitches, assist in tweaking the systems and customize practices to meet their specific needs. On paper, literally and figuratively, these tools are very black and white. In real life, you may need to add a lot of your own creative thinking and preferences to make them work for you. That's perfect, if that's what works best for you. No matter what, it's got to work for you.

Whether you are ready to feast on this content or feel a bit overwhelmed, one of the many benefits of this book is that you can take your time. Refer back to specific sections when you find yourself repeating old, unproductive habits, bumping up against obstacles or feeling like life is moving too fast, again. Dog ear it, highlight it, tab it. Stickie the hell out of it! Share it with your friends, Intruders and Distractors. The practices in this book will support you in achieving the goals you really desire, while building the calm, orderly life you've always wanted.

A Few Final Words

What a journey we just traveled together. The closer I came to completing this book, the more one word kept coming up, Resilience. When I sat down to start this book, I was full of passion, fire, creative energy and determination. My right brain, the very analytical, process oriented part, was fully engaged and firing. I was hyper-focused and supercharged. Nothing could get in my way.

Then, life happened. My energy tanked, several times, and the goal of writing this book lost its top billing status. However, it was never far from my mind. I kept sharing the goal with my community forcing me to be public and accountable to the task at hand. In the low times I'd think, "As soon as I feel better I'll get back to it." Energy would return and I'd assess what I needed to do to dig in again. Sometimes I had to take tiny steps, writing just a couple of paragraphs a week. Other times I'd recognize I needed an accountability partner, someone to check in with and assure that I was putting in the writing time. Finally, when it got near the end, it required completely clearing my calendar for a few days. Those final days I could taste success and it was very heady!

Not surprisingly, I called on what I had learned about myself during this writing and goal setting process over and over again. *I learned that I do my best work at* Panera. Why? I can't be distracted by household chores or well-meaning friends and family. I learned to combine my daily exercise routine with my need to leave the house, by riding the three miles each way to Panera to write.

Through the whole journey, the ups and downs, and the dry spells, I continued to remind myself that I had decided this was a priority. As such, I needed to find the stuff to keep going.

Resilience. Showing up again and again. No matter what life throws in your way. What I learned from writing this book is that I am resilient; and, you are too. Resilience is what makes you get up in the morning and go to work when life is… life. It will always be somewhat messy; and you may be momentarily distracted from your goal; your plans may be derailed by forces beyond your control. If your goal is truly a priority, you will have to find whatever it takes to begin again and again and again.

Success. It's a new feeling for me, feeling success. I am considered, by most, to be an accomplished person. Yet, experiencing the joy of success is new to me. What I have learned is that when you take the time to recognize the milestones you've set for yourself and celebrate that success, you begin to build a foundation of positivity and strength. The constant yearning subsides and all you are left with is the joy of a job well done, a unique sense of expansiveness that may or may not need to be filled.

The only limit to the height of your achievements is the reach of your dreams and your willingness to work for them.
Michelle Obama.

When you understand how you think about goals, you begin to understand: how you think about life; what motivates you; what kind of support you need; and where your weaknesses are. You begin to make allowances and accommodations, and capitalize on your strengths. When you understand this, success is the only possible

240

outcome, because you have planned for it. No matter what small piece of delicious guidance you take from this book, you are better of now than you were before. You know yourself better than you did before. For that effort you get to celebrate. Because you are amazing and

You've got this.

With love,
Lisa

Want more Lisa in your life?
Sign up today for your daily gentle reminder to stay focused on your Game Changer goals in a calm, productive manner with Lisa's monthly subscription program Game Changer Mornings. Detail can be found at www.LisaStearns.com

One to One Coaching and Dream Team Mastermind™ Groups, www.LisaStearns.com

Co-hosted, weekly Just One Thing podcast, JustOneThing.Buzzsprout.com

Reflections on my Journey:
What I've learned about myself that I love.
What I've learned about myself to help me grow.

_____

_____

_____

_____

_____

_____

_____

_____

_____

_____

_____

_____

_____

_____

_____

_____

_____

_____

_____

Section 6

The Nitty Gritty

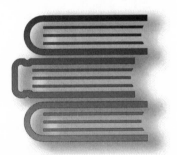

References & Resources

Action Words to Clarify Tasks & Goals

advertise

advise

analyze

assign

attain/get

catalog

clarify

collect

compile

compose

communicate

complete

condense

consolidate

contribute

coordinate

consult

contact

decide

define

describe

delegate

develop

direct

discuss

edit

eliminate

expand

file

gather

hire

identify

improve

inform

inspect

join

lead

listen

locate

log

make

manage

market

measure

merge

negotiate

observe

obtain

order

organize

outline

overhaul

plan

print

prioritize

produce

publicize

recruit

register

repair

replace

research

respond

resolve

review

schedule

set up

study

submit

summarize

supervise

systemize

upgrade

verify

write

The Nitty-Gritty:
References & Resources

Works Cited
Ben-Shahar, Tal, *Happier: Learn the Secrets to Daily Joy and Lasting Fulfillment.* McGraw-Hill 2007

Grover, Sean, Do You Have a Controlling Personality?, *Psychology Today Blog*, Nov. 30, 2017

Hay, Louise, *You Can Heal Your Life.* Hay House 2004

Hill, Napoleon, *Think and Grow Rich.* The Ralston Society, Meriden, Conn. Original Copyright 1937

Additional Sources:
SMART Goals:
Drucker, Peter, *Management by Objectives.*
First published usage: Doran, George T., *Management Review.* November 1981 issue.

Readiness Chart
Prochaska, JO; DiClemente, CC. *The Transtheoretical Approach: Crossing Traditional Boundaries of Therapy.* Homewood, IL: Dow Jones-Irwin; 1983

That's all, folks! :-)

Things I Want to Remember